ISBN 978-1-334-22222-1
PIBN 10587230

For support please visit www.forgottenbooks.com

English
Français
Deutsche
Italiano
Español
Português

www.forgottenbooks.com

Mythology Photography **Fiction**
Fishing Christianity **Art** Cooking
Essays Buddhism Freemasonry
Medicine **Biology** Music **Ancient
Egypt** Evolution Carpentry Physics
Dance Geology **Mathematics** Fitness
Shakespeare **Folklore** Yoga Marketing
Confidence Immortality Biographies
Poetry **Psychology** Witchcraft
Electronics Chemistry History **Law**
Accounting **Philosophy** Anthropology
Alchemy Drama Quantum Mechanics
Atheism Sexual Health **Ancient History**
Entrepreneurship Languages Sport
Paleontology Needlework Islam
Metaphysics Investment Archaeology
Parenting Statistics Criminology
Motivational

The Greatest Event in Canadian
History

The
Battle of the Plains

BY

J. M. HARPER

Author of "Champlain: a Drama," "The Montgomery Siege," "The Prince's Booklet,"
"Sacrament Sunday," "Songs of
the Commonwealth," etc.

TORONTO
THE MUSSON BOOK COMPANY
LIMITED

TO MY FRIEND
COLONEL J. FERDINAND TURNBULL
LATE INSPECTOR OF CAVALRY
AND
PRESIDENT OF THE GARRISON CLUB

CONTENTS

Prefatory Note .

THE Battle of the Plains of Abraham stands out as a memorable event in the history of the world, being not only the most important event in the history of Canada, but an achievement of the highest moment in the military annals of the British Empire as well. And the celebration of its occurrence on the immediate outskirts of the city of Quebec, by the issue of such a volume as this, cannot but be of interest to the King's subjects in every part of the British possessions. The battle in question is sandwiched between two collateral events, namely, the Repulse at Montmorency and the Battle of Sainte-Foye; and within the scope of this memorial volume, an unambitious attempt is made to bring its readers in touch with the topography of the scenes of these conflicts, by means of a series of observation lessons, having each for its nucleus a synopsis in verse, *à là ballade*,—the said ballads being supplemented by notes explanatory of each event, recorded in the order of its happening, and the whole being given to the public as an authentic account of the Third Siege of Quebec, on the one hundred and fiftieth year after its occurrence.

General Introduction

As there are three main events in one to be remembered in connection with the Siege of Quebec in 1759-60, so there are three main vantage-points, among many others in that city, from which observations may most conveniently be made of the battlefields connected therewith in turn. The first of these three events of the siege was the unsuccessful assault made by General Wolfe at the eastern end of General Montcalm's line of defence, which extended all the way from the city to the Montmorency River; and the scene of that assault may be studied to the greatest advantage from the city end of the Dufferin Terrace, or from one of the windows of the Chateau Frontenac. The inner extremity of the Island of Orleans, with its nestling village and church spire, forms a picturesque landmark of the first landing-place of Wolfe's army, on the arrival of the British fleet up the channel to the left of the island looking up the river. Secondly, the scenes connected with the preliminary driftings of the fleet up and down the river, before Wolfe and his army had arrived on the battlefield proper to the rear of the town, may be scanned with like convenience from the remote end of the extended Dufferin Terrace, as it finds its exit into the Battlefields Park beyond the Citadel's western trenches; and, thirdly, the topog-

11

raphy of the battlefield itself, on which the Battle of the Plains and the Battle of Sainte-Foye were successively fought, can best be studied from the mound behind the spot where the English general breathed his last, or from the tower of the Franciscan Convent.

Some visitors have been known to plume themselves on having "done" Quebec in a forenoon, in a day or two, in a week; but a full summer's residence in the place, or even a lifetime's, is hardly sufficient for a properly exhaustive study of what Matthew Arnold once called, in the hearing of the writer, the Edinburgh of Canada.   Nor is there any more convenient spot in the whole city from which a first lesson may be learned of the topography of the more striking points of interest, old or new, than on or near the site of Champlain's Monument and the Dufferin Terrace.   There, it may safely be said, one stands upon the most romantically interesting spot in the whole of Canada, if not of the continent of America—where a first Governor of Canada built a first stronghold for himself and the pioneers that were of his clientele, and which, historically speaking, was for two centuries or more, to the city of Quebec what Quebec has been to the whole country.   Here originated the most momentous colonial movements of the old regime under French rulers, and of the new regime under British rulers.   And, if one would know thoroughly and well the topography of this old town, as an initiation to the study of its annals, imperial and provincial, not omitting its ecclesiastical, philanthropic, and industrial developments, no more advantageously interesting a spot could be selected, as has been said, for a start in the study, than the promenade round the face of Cape Diamond,

from the site of the old Chien d'Or towards the western
limits of the new park.

In a word, that unrivalled public promenade stands
as the most convenient of all base-lines in the city,
from which the intelligent observer may at once dis-
cern Quebec's justifiable ranking among the cities
of world-wide interest—one from which the student
of history may happily enter upon a course of prac-
tical paideutics all by himself, that well might be
taken up with advantage by more of the schools in
the Empire, in their historical curricula. Topograph-
ical and geographical studies should always go hand-
in-hand with historical studies; and nowhere can that
pedagogical doctrine be better illustrated than during
a right kind of a visit paid to Quebec and its environs.
Here in presence of nearly every phase of the picturesque, one may study out the *raison d'être* of historic evolutions from the colonial experiences of the
pioneer, through the aggrandizements of the seigneur,
into the fuller freedom of rule by majorities and equal
rights. Or, rather, if the romantic should happen to
be more in line with the predilections of the visitor
who would study history on the spot, may it not well
be asked where could there be found such a blending
of the traditional and the romantic in the simple life,
than along the country highways radiating from the
promenade of Cape Diamond, or such a blending of
tradition and romance as may be met with in the annals of those who, springing from the old *noblesse* of
former times, have made a history of its own, and a
social status as well, for this, the oldest city in Canada? Nor, indeed, can it be looked upon as a waste
of time on the part of the writer to bestow a paragraph-

length or two, to emphasize the marvel of this vantage-promenade of Quebec, which is about to be supplemented by one of the most spacious battlefield parks in the world, with its main drive running from the city across the tracts of land where were fought the Battle of the Plains and the Battle of Sainte-Foye, and back again by another route.

The promenade in question was opened to the public in 1879, by the Earl of Dufferin, then Governor-General of Canada. The Chateau St. Louis, which had been a residence for French governors and English governors for over two centuries, was accidentally destroyed by fire in Lord Aylmer's time; and, for all of four years, its walls begrimed with smoke stood as an eyesore near the spot where the striking Champlain monument now stands, within the shadow of the palatial Chateau Frontenac. To bury out of sight the ruins of this tough old structure, whose foundation walls are still to be traced, Lord Durham, who succeeded Lord Aylmer, suggested that a platform be raised over the spot; and, in 1838, in accordance with his further wishes, that platform was developed into a spacious promenade, overlooking the Old Parliament Building and the slope of Mountain Street. The writer interestingly remembers making his earliest observations of the magnificent harbour and its outer environment, and the quaint streets and buildings of the lower town, from that somewhat ruinous-looking prospect-point, in 1868, thirty years after it had first been opened to the public, and three years before it came into the ownership of the provincial and civic authorities for safe-keeping. Finally, under what was called the "Dufferin Improvement Scheme" for the beautifying of the city, the Durham Terrace was extended as far as the base of the King's Bastion, and had its name changed to the name it now goes by, namely, the Dufferin Terrace; and, later, this was further supplemented by a less substantial extension, at the instance of Sir Wilfrid Laurier, Premier of Canada—the whole structure as it stands to-day being over half a mile in length. To add to the attractiveness of its environment, it has in its rear the Chateau Frontenac, the Governor's Garden and the outer wall of the Citadel, within the second of these being a well-shaded and grateful retreat, impressively adorned by the monument to Wolfe and Montcalm, bearing for its superscription the following concise bit of Latin, conjointly referring to the two heroes of the event of September the 13th, 1759:

MORTEM. VIRTUS. COMMUNEM.
FAMAM. VICTORIA.
MONUMENTUM. POSTERITAS
DEDIT.

an aphorism from the pen of Dr. John Charlton Fisher, and a record in marble of the change of imperial masters for the colony.

And, summer or winter, in daylight or darkness, the gifted visitor to the city is always finding some new inspiration from the spot where

Of choice escaped awhile from commerce cares,
The memory cradled on the velvet charms
Of nature, hums its olden song, and plays
With history's fingers to assure the tune;

or where, when the sun has retired for the day, and
companionship seeks its solace amid the crowding
citizens, one becomes more and more engrossed in
the scene,

> Within a flood of festive light that glares
> A dazzling nucleus 'mid encircling gloom,
> Where earth below seems heaven for brilliancy
> That twinkles in the landscape and the glass
> Of waters gleaming like a nether sky.

And what Howells has said of the spot in its summer
aspects, the morning newspaper of the city once took
time to tell us what it looks like in winter.

The former in his "Wedding Journey" has told us
how the locality impressed him at that particular
moment of eventide, when the valleys and the heights
around were vanishing after sunset. The river de-
fines itself, he says, by the varicoloured lights of the
ships and steamers that lie dark and motionless hulks
upon its broad breast. The lights of Levis swarm
upon the other shore. The lower town, two hundred
feet below, stretches along an alluring mystery of
clustering roofs and lamp-lit windows, and dark and
shining streets around the mighty rock, mural crowned.
Suddenly a long arch lightens over the northern hori-
zon; the tremulous flames of the aurora, pallid violet
or faintly tinged with crimson, shoot upwards from
it and play with a vivid apparition and evanescence
to the zenith. And while one looks and looks to wonder at the phenomena, a gun booms from the Citadel,
and the wild sweet notes of the bugle spring out from
the silence.

Nor one whit less true or striking is what the equally

gifted writer in the Quebec newspaper, whose name is now undiscoverable, says of the look of things in winter, from this entrancingly engrossing vantage outlook. A magnificent picture it is, he says, a most magnificent picture, a scene of glorified nature painted by the hand of the Creator himself. The setting sun has charged the skies with all the gorgeous heraldry of purple and crimson and gold, and the tints are diffused and reflected through fleecy clouds becoming softer and softer through expansion. The mountain tops, wood-crowned, where the light and shadow struggle for mastery, stand out in relief, with the deep blue of the clear waters beyond, from which the Island of Orleans rises, and into which its nearest promontory juts out in rural picturesqueness. The light plays through the frost-adorned but still sombre pines, and spreads out over the deserted fields. Levis and the south shore of the river receive their share of that light, while the grimness of the Citadel serves as a contrast and a relief to the eye, bewildered with the exceptional splendour of things terrestrial. But, as the sun sinks deeper behind the eternal hills, shadows begin to lengthen, and the bright colours gradually tone down to the grey of dusk. The stars shine out, the grey is chased away, and the azure diamond-dotted skies tell not of the glory of sunset which has so shortly before suffused them.

And yet the story is only half told in these brilliant descriptions of the blending of natural beauty and historic interest that hallows this vantage height for observation, when it is viewed in itself from the Citadel above and the harbour below, in the light of the advances that have been made towards its fuller beautification and illumination, in these later times of tasteful architecture and electric lighting. What a fairy tale the nucleus of the environment illustrates, when it is lit up of a night in all its brilliancy, as

> Two streams of gayety go tripping past,
> Now here, now there, timing their gladsome pace,
> To music's strains that sweeten friendship's hour,
> And mingle with the whispered tale of love,
> Soft breathed and coy in ear of blushing maid,
> Or yet renewed to joy the matron's cares!

What a charm there is in it all, as an accompaniment to the traditions and memorials of early colonial life, with which the place seems to teem, as well as to the historical setting of the great turning-point event which brought British and French within the influence of a common patriotism and citizenship under the Union Jack! Can the Empire boast of many such rallying points surpassing in interest to this one, outside of London and Edinburgh and Dublin and the other largest cities of the British Isles—any such a holiday rendezvous for its citizens, any such living memorial of loyalty and national exploitation? Nay, is there any more of an appropriate place in the wide world where the British subject, or even the visitor from outside the Empire, may learn a never to be forgotten lesson on history, such as is the one we have in hand in this volume?

BELOW THE FALLS OF MONTMORENCY

The Repulse at Montmorency

THE FIRST CONTEST

Introduction to First Contest

FROM the city end of the Dufferin Terrace, possibly from under one of its several kiosks, the whole plan of Wolfe's first attempt to bring Montcalm out into the open for battle can be read from the landscape, beginning with the little parish church of Petronille on the Island of Orleans, where was the first camping-ground of the British troops, and where the British general first directed his field-glass against the long line of the city's defences up from the Beauport beach. When the tidings was carried to Quebec that the British were on their way up the river, the authorities of the place made hurried preparations to present a fortified front to the invaders; and, though Montcalm's suggestion, to fortify the approaches to the rear as well as on both sides of the river, was over-ruled, on the plea that the British vessels were not likely to run the gauntlet of the Citadel batteries and those lower down on the front of the cliff, everything was done that could be done in the time to strengthen the approaches by way of Beauport and the river front. Indeed, the walls of the city, except down by Palace Gate, had been left in a state of neglect from the time of the first Vaudreuil. And, seeing that no reliance was to be placed in their condition to resist a siege, it was decided by the French that the entrance to the

St. Charles River should be blocked by a boom, with
a floating battery in front, and that an inner bridge
of boats should be erected as a means of bringing troops
from Beauport, if the emergency arose of checking
an advance of the enemy from behind. In the rear
of the residence of Ringfield on the road to Charlesbourg, there may still be seen the outlines of the great
circumvallation or horn-work, which Montcalm's engineers had scooped out as a place of retreat for the
French troops, should the necessity for retreat arise;
and from this circular camping ground, capable of
sheltering from two to three thousand men, a line of
redoubts commanded by two, three, or four guns each,
were erected at every likely landing-place along the
shore-line—such landing-places being still to be identified in a rough way, in a line parallel with the highway that now forms the continuous street of the long
village of Beauport, as one may see it to-day from
the parapet of the Dufferin Terrace.

Behind this fortified line there were stationed at
intervals a mixed armament of fifteen or sixteen thousand regulars, militia, and volunteers, Montcalm's
army having been augmented, as soon as the word
went round the parishes that Wolfe was approaching,
by crowds of men and lads, in answer to Governor
Vaudreuil's demands for all the men of fighting age
who could possibly be brought together to withstand
the enemy. As soon as the prospect of a siege was
pledged, Montcalm took up his headquarters at the
Beauport Manor House, the site of which is plainly
discernible from the Dufferin Terrace, and Vaudreuil
immediately afterwards forsook his residence in the
city to take up his quarters alongside of the General.

In the city there was left a garrison of about a thousand men under the command of Chevalier de Ramézay, all the city gates being closed, with the exception of Palace Gate, which, with its near approaches strengthened more than were those of the other gates, was left open as a ready exit for the detachments on their way to the bridge of boats.

Montcalm's line of defence thus extended from Ringfield all the way to the Montmorency, and from Ringfield by the way of the fortified boom across the St. Charles, to the city's walls, the right wing, centred near what is now known as La Canardière, or duck-feeding ground, to the west of the site of the Beauport Asylum, being in charge of Chevalier de St. Ours, and the left wing at Montmorency in charge of Chevalier de Lévis. Thus had those in authority, ignoring for the most part the danger that might spring up in the rear of the city, made strong their position in Beauport; and when it is seen from the topography of the place, that the Levis side of the river was as much in need of being fortified as the Beauport side, it is not difficult to locate the mistake which General Wolfe, not having it pertinently in his mind from the first, took advantage of later, when he found it impossible to force the Montmorency wing of his adversary's army or any other part of it, stretched out as it was into the city along a distance of over seven miles.

In a word, it was the repulse at Montmorency that brought Wolfe face to face with his opponent's self-conscious mistake. In venturing to challenge De Lévis at Montmorency,· he had thought that Montcalm, fearing the onset against his left wing, would have concentrated his forces towards its support, and

thus have presented his antagonist with the opportunity of attacking him in the rear as well as in front,
if only a section of the British troops could safely be
hurried across the river by way of the upper ford,
while the Grenadiers and the Royal Americans were
forcing their way up the nearest Montmorency slopes
to the west of the ford below the Falls. But the impetuosity of these detachments was an immediate
mistake that ruined the prospect of such a general
fore-and-aft engagement. And while Wolfe lectured
these reckless fighters for their heedlessness, he had
to confess on his own part, in his dispatches, that even
had the attack below the Falls been successful, the
loss of life on the British side would have been very
great, and that even had the projected attack on the
rear been likewise successful, the River St. Charles
would still have had to be crossed, before the town
itself could have been invested in a close siege.

Before Wolfe had been fully seized with the idea
of the advantage there was to him in the French not
fortifying the Levis heights as they had the Beauport
shore, thus leaving the way open to the invader should
he make up his mind to remove his Levis camp from
the bend of the St. Lawrence further up that river,
his thoughts seem to have been busied over two alternatives, as a means of immediate success. Admiral
Saunders and he were of one mind as to the necessity
of forcing Montcalm out into the open, there to pit
army against army; and even after his repulse at the
Falls, he still kept pondering the problem of future
attack, with the north shore in his eye as the scene of
his efforts. Even after he had examined the St. Lawrence above, and some of the Admiral's ships had

succeeded in eluding the city's batteries, Wolfe returned to his camp on the Island of Orleans, to rum-
inate over his two alternatives. One of these was to
land with a heavy force against Montcalm's centre,
near the mouth of one of the Beauport streams, and
there bring on a general engagement. The other was
to march the bulk of his army across the Montmorency
by the upper ford, and come on Montcalm from behind. But Admiral Saunders, with full faith in the
correctness of Shipmaster's Cook soundings (see Note),
told his colleague that it would be utterly impossible
for any of his ships to sail near enough to the Beauport
shore-line, to land troops or to cover them in their
advance up to the enemy's line, after the redoubts
had been demolished or forsaken; and the lesson
learned at the lower ford of the Montmorency was
too recent for any one to think of daring a repetition
of the carnage that befell the Grenadiers and the Royal
Americans in that engagement. This first alternative
had therefore to be laid aside. The second alternative, namely, that of taking troops across by the upper
ford, was likewise proven to be as hazardous as the
first alternative, and when these two alternatives were
finally dismissed from the General's mind, there was
nothing for him to do but force his way up the main
river, and there seek the easiest landing to the levels
behind the city. Thus indirectly he would force Montcalm to forsake his formidable trenches and redoubts
at Beauport, in order to find his way into the city by
way of his bridge of boats, for its immediate protection.
   The mistake of not having fortified the Levis side
of the St. Lawrence had by this time begun to dawn
upon those who had set aside Montcalm's suggestion

about fortifying the open spaces in the rear of the town. Wolfe claims, in one of his despatches, that the dangers of his advancing up the Levis side of the main river had been increased, from the attention which the besieged had been giving to this line of approach. "I found there great difficulties," he says, "arising from the nature of the ground, and the obstacles to our communication with the fleet. But what I feared most was that, if we should land between the river and Cap Rouge, the body first landed would not be reinforced before they were attacked by the enemy's whole army. Notwithstanding these difficulties, I thought once of attempting it, but perceiving that the enemy, jealous of the design, were preparing against it, and had actually brought artillery, which, being so near Quebec, they could increase as they pleased, to play upon the shipping, and as it must have been hours before we could attack them, even supposing a favourable night for the boats to pass by the town unhurt, it seemed so hazardous that I thought it best to desist."

Meantime, however, in spite of the danger and the gloom of sickness and disappointment that could not but be settling on Wolfe's mind, the St. Lawrence above the town became the scene of operations supplementary to the bombardment that knew little interruption from the Levis batteries and those of the fleet. Bougainville had been despatched from Beauport to Cap Rouge with a large detachment and four guns. Brigadier-General Murray was also up in this quarter with a large force on the opposite side of the river. Several vessels, French and British, were likewise to be seen moving up and down with the tide, above and below Cap Rouge. Yet, for all this, Wolfe remained in the vicinity of the mouth of the Montmorency. The feebleness of approaching death was upon him, as he lay in a farm-house near the headquarters of Brigadier-General Townshend, who was to some extent first in command on that side. "I know perfectly well you cannot cure me," said he to the doctor in attendance on him; "but pray make me up so that I may be without pain for a few days and able to do my duty; that is all I want." And then from his next despatch we learn that, after consulting with Monckton and his other officers, he acquiesced in the proposal to make an attempt on the rear of the town, taking his whole army with him, except what would leave the camps on the Island of Orleans and at the bend of the St. Lawrence in a proper state of defence.

The Repulse at Montmorency

The pains of war, the bliss of peace, how come
    they e'er to be
Co-ordinates of glory, in a world of God's de-
    cree?
Is't the striving or the bitterness in victory· and
    defeat,
That makes the pæans of the past a sanctity so
    sweet,
To the nations in their loud acclaim of the blend-
    ing of the two,
In the annals of attainment, incentive to the new?

'Twas a world's conflagration,[1] with the world
    looking on,
That sent its faggots, red with rage, across the
    Atlantic zone;
'Twas Britain, segregating from her allies, sailed
    the seas,
To assure colonial prowess, a-running to the
    lees;[2]
And the striving, void of bitterness, to-day we
    celebrate,
In the unity of nationhood eliminate of hate.

What a crowning to our country is our garlanding
    of peace![3]

3   29

'Tis the victory last of victories, giving *amitié*
    release;
Making brotherhood of counsel, as reversal and
    success
We read of in the record, with no bias to caress;[4]
Making blessing of the wars that were, in the peace
    that now prevails—
God's blessing on our loyalty as every wounding
    heals.

"I bring you," said the invader, "a royal master's
    word:[5]
"'Tis the curbing of the oppressor that edges Eng-
    land's sword.
"The protection of the British flag 'twere folly to
    refuse,
"Since the getting rid of tyrants has in it naught
    to lose:
"There's no deception in my hand, only a sword
    to save,
"From the callousness of masters who would your
    freedom reave."

"I have no warrant to molest the toilers on the
    land;
"Neither peaceful priest nor peasant are we here
    with woe to brand;
"My men are armed to avenge your wrongs, not to
    lay waste your homes:
"Nay, the rights of all non-combatants are safe
    when victory comes.
"To you the hand of friendship old England now
    extends.
"While what is hurtful to us all she valorous for-
    fends."

But the answer to the message runs along the Beau-
    port shore,
By a measuring of distance and a threatening in
    its roar:
"We are ready for your coming,"[6] that answer
    seems to say,
"So gird your loins, *mes braves anglais*, with no
    lingering for the fray:
"We seek no king of England as master in New
    France,
"Proud Louis is our sovereign, our fealty no mis-
    chance."

"This land is his and ours, assured by deed of prior
    claim:
"Thrice have you sought to wrest it, and thrice
    have suffered shame:
"If our rulers have been profligate, to bring on us
    disgrace,
"We may not stain our loyalty, to stultify the base.
"Our Montcalm and De Lévis, defiant as the tide,
"Can hurl reprisal at your king, however he may
    chide."

And the gage of war is soon ta'en up by the ad-
    miral of the fleet,[7]
While the General still weighs counsel with a sol-
    dier's skill discreet:
A cloud of expectation lies a-brooding o'er the bay,
As foresight plans its cautions from ominous day
    to day,
With camps located, three in turn,[8] to watch Mont-
    calm's defence,[9]
Until the moment calls alarm to compass war's
    advance.

The fleet makes sure its soundings,[10] as a prelude
    to the storm
Of shot and shell on town and fort, to implement
    alarm;
While the Island camp sends strong relays along
    the Levis heights,
And east of Montmorency where the cataract
    crinites;
And all the while Montcalm looks on with eye
    importunate,
To muster strength wherever Wolfe assault may
    concentrate.

And well the latter knows success is only his afield,
Where battle-line dares battle-line, till either has
    to yield;
And long he scans the outlet-ford,[11] to find a mar-
    gin-space
Whereon his men may footing find, the enemy to
    face,
Guarding as well the eastern bank, from upper-ford
    to strand,[12]
Each outpost placed within redoubt, and Town-
    shend in command.[13]

Nor is his rival heedless of the tactics of the foe,
As strength for strength he shrewd locates, behind
    each hillock's brow;
Having thought of crossing from above, to drive
    the invader back,
To the channel or Ange Gardien,[14] to rout all side
    attack;
Ne'er forgetting concentration when the main as-
    sault is made,
To force a way on Beauport Flats by preconcerted
    raid.

And the singing of the centuries[15] is in our wistful
 ear,
As the cataract keeps a-rhyming the story of the
 year;
When its prehistoric routine was disturbed by
 battle-storm,
Where its silvered wreathings wimple out, in rip-
 ples retiform,
As if 'twere brooklet once again, before it runs
 aglee,
Into the great St. Lawrence and its broadening
 to the sea.

In its awe-inspiring presence, we can read the tale
 anew,
How a counter rage of torrents across its torrent
 flew;
Repentigny daring Townshend,[16] from his shelter-
 ings from above;
The *Centurion* issuing challenge,[17] to De Lévis'
 every move;
While Murray waits the signal, the lower ford to
 ward,
As the Grenadiers intrepid rush over the spray-wet
 sward.

Will they silence the approaches, and disarm the
 near redoubt?
Is there field enough for two brigades, when beyond the ford they're brought?
Behold the Grenadiers advance,[18] beyond the outer
 breach,
Heedless of danger, out of rank, beyond precaution's reach!
God grant they meet no dire mishap, in their reckless raid pell-mell!

God save us! See! They're driven back from before the mouth of hell!

For the defenders of the entrenchments, well-counselled in their zeal,
Have waited, hardly breathing, their presence to conceal,
Till the Grenadiers, outrun of fear, their ready victims stand,
On the inner edge of danger, in range of death's demand:
Mowed down like grass from the sting of hail, a remnant turns to flee,
With all re-forming past control, even under Monckton's eye.[19]

Ah! who will brave the danger now, though the batteries all around—
From the ships near by, to the heights above—defiance still propound?
Is there climbing for the vanguard, with its footing now on land?
Is there chance for open contest, from the gorge-slope to the strand?
The night is fast approaching, the wind bewinged a gale,
The tide outruns its turning, the rain weaves shredded pall:[20]

Yet the bugle sounds defiance still, as Murray forms his line,
And Townshend sends advance to cross the ford below the chine,

While the rescued of the Grenadiers creep for shel-
    ter near the shore,
Where the faithful plead for rallying, as misfor-
    tune they deplore;
Ay, even while Montcalm's keen *qui vive* keeps up
    a fierce reply,
From the thickets that o'erlook the strand, in blasts
    of musketry.

And still the cataract evolves, supreme in such a
    scene,
As if 'twere Godhead looking on, at the stridency
    of men.
Is there glory in such slaughter? Is this defiance
    sane?
Bears this masterpiece of courage the forehead
    mark of Cain?
"Were it not humane to counsel pause," the tur-
    moil seems to say,
"Since nature maketh laughter of all this war-
    array?"

"'Since nature maketh laughter!' What mean
    you by the phrase?
"Laughter at man and courage, the pride of glory's
    days?"
Nay, then, 'tis but the cataract enhancing war's
    demand,
As General Wolfe, with prudence, sounds retreat
    on every hand:
"The foe is worthy of our steel, with advantage
    on his side,
"And spare we must the lives of men, whatever
    may betide."

And now there's passive heed of call, Townshend
    the first to obey,
With the wind and rain benighting the deepening
    grey of day:
The bateaux soon are laden with Murray's men
    on board,
The Royals and the Grenadiers,[21] with shame
    within them stirred:
Nor was there purpose of pursuit, no sign of dire
    retreat,
Only imprudence suffering check, with glory from
    the feat.

It seems the general's orders—Montcalm's and
    Wolfe's alike—
Were overlooked throughout the day from impul-
    siveness and pique—[22]
The Grenadiers, in hazard outrunning all restraint,
The crossing of the ford above delayed by envy's
    plaint—
But the "might have been" ne'er amplifies the
    facts of history,
To turn the scale when the balance weighs the
    eclat of bravery.

The escapade was prelude to the issue of the war,
But the testing of a purpose with victory still afar:
The fame of Montcalm claims foresight, as com-
    panion to his skill,
While Wolfe's renown for prudence is a best in
    courage still:
Yea, such prelude, like the victory, gives us tab-
    leau of the twain,
As a brave man and a brave man, under heroic
    strain.

And the singing of the centuries is in our wistful
    ear,
As the cataract keeps a-rhyming the story of the
    year;
When its prehistoric routine was disturbed by
    battle-storm,
Where its silvered wreathings wimple out, in rip-
    ples retiform,
As if 'twere brooklet once again, to tell us all aglee
Of the part it played in the long ago as a child of
    history.

Notes on "The Repulse at Montmorency"

1. *"'Twas a world's conflagration."* The Seven Years' War began in 1756, with the invasion of Saxony by Frederick the Great, the European allies against him being Austria, Russia, and France, with Great Britain as an ally in his favour. The challenge which Britain threw down to France in the same year was an outcome of the former's alliance with Prussia, and had for one of its main objects the upholding of the dominancy of British rule in the colonies of America—an object finally gained by the taking of Louisbourg in 1758, and the capture of Quebec in 1759. Meanwhile Britain shared largely in the general fighting in Europe, supporting at its own charge what was known as the British Hanoverian Army under the command of Duke Ferdinand of Brunswick, whose skill as a commander was duly endorsed by the victories of Crefelt and Minden. Beyond this, Britain asserted her supremacy on the seas, by her successes in America and India, with the naval victories of Quiberon and Belleisle crowning her other achievements. In 1760, George III died, and the subsidies for carrying on the war in alliance with Frederick ceased. In 1762, the Czarina of Russia died, leaving the government of that country in the hands of Peter III, grandson of Peter the Great, who was personally a warm admirer of Frederick. Austria's resources for the moment were all but exhausted, and peace seemed to come of itself in 1763, under the terms of the Treaty of Paris. The chief provisions of that treaty included a re-arrangement of colonial possessions, Britain being awarded all of Canada and the territory east of the Mississippi, with the exception of Louisiana; and France having some of her property restored to her in the Indies and in Africa. The war in Canada was brought to an end on the 8th of September, 1760, when Vaudreuil was forced to make a formal surrender of the whole country to Generals Amherst and Murray, three years before the Treaty of Paris was signed.

2. *"Colonial prowess a-running to the lees."* The great main story of early Canadian history has to do with the French and English rivalries in America. At the time of Wolfe's invasion there were about seventy thousand Frenchmen in America to a million of Englishmen; and misgivings had arisen in the minds of the people of Great Britain, that neither the Duke of Newcastle, as premier, nor his American generals, were ever likely to secure the ascendancy of the New England colonies in the struggle between them and their French rivals north of them. These generals—Loudon, Webb, and Abercrombie—have been set down by Sir Gilbert Parker as vain and obtuse martinets, who fumbled their opportunities, mismanaged their campaigns, and learned no lessons from their failures. And, be this as it may, Montcalm had certainly worked wonders in the west against their movements by seizing Fort Frontenac, reducing Oswego, and capturing Fort William Henry, until, at last, the indignation in England became such that Newcastle had to resign in favour of William Pitt, who made no delay in placing the military operations in North America in the hands of such men as Amherst, Wolfe and Howe.

3. *"Our garlanding of peace."* When the inauguration of a Battlefields Park for Quebec was first mooted, it was suggested that a "Monument of Peace" should be erected somewhere near the King's Bastion, which might be seen as a prominent historic landmark to those arriving up the St. Lawrence, much as is to be seen the Bartholdi "Statue to Liberty" by those sailing across the harbour of New York. The originator of the idea was Earl Grey, who took such a prominent part, with the Prince of Wales and Lord Roberts, in the Tercentennial celebrations of 1908.

4. *"With no bias to caress."* Many are prone to make too much of a taken-for-granted racial antipathy between the French-speaking and English-speaking citizens of Canada. There are certainly no grounds for any such an antipathy, unless it be in the desire to aggrandize beyond the lines of political equity and civic privilege. As a part of the British Empire, Canada maintains the principle of "equal rights" for all her citizens.

5. *"I bring you a royal master's word."* General Wolfe reached the Island of Orleans on June 27th, 1759, where he ordered his

troops to disembark and provide for a central camp in full view
of the Falls of Montmorency. Two days afterwards, he issued
a manifesto to the Canadians, a copy of which he caused to be
placed on the door of the nearest church. The substance of that
manifesto is given in the stanza from which the above is quoted.
The purpose of his invasion, as he said, was to take away from
the crown of France, a colonial oversight which had inflicted so
many wrongs on the English colonists in America, without bene-
fiting to any large extent the colonists of New France.   The
King of England, in fact, had heard of the calamitous condition
of affairs along the settlements of the St. Lawrence, and was willing to provide a remedy, should his offers of protection and friendship be accepted by the inhabitants of New France. In a word,
the manifesto promised a generous amnesty to all who would
abstain from taking part in the war, finally closing with the sen-
tence: "Let all Canadians consult, in this matter, their own good
with prudence: their future lot now depends on their own choice."

6. *"We are ready for your coming."* Such a reply finds historical authentification only from the after conduct of the peasantry
of the country, who flocked from all parts to join Montcalm, until
there were crowded into Quebec and its Beauport outposts over
sixteen thousand men prepared to withstand the invader.

7. *"The admiral of the fleet."* Admiral Saunders and the other
naval officers of his staff, as soon as Wolfe's army had been disembarked on the Island of Orleans, lost no time in arranging for
the stations which their respective vessels should assume, and in
testing the distances from the shore for bombarding purposes.
The British fleet formed one of the strongest and most effective
elements in the siege, there having been on board its vessels sundry subalterns who afterwards reached the acme of fame as officers of the British navy. Among these may be mentioned Midshipman Jervis, afterwards Admiral St. Vincent; second, that
intrepid captain of the ship of the line *Mercury*, afterwards Admiral Palliser; and third, the sailing-master of the same vessel,
who afterwards made a world-wide fame as Captain Cook, the
distinguished circumnavigator.

8. *"With camps located three in turn."*   The main camp of Wolfe's army was situated near the site of what is now the parish church of Petronille, with a redoubt of two guns near the beach, just below where the church stands.   The second camp was situated on the headland near the site of the dry-dock, with a redoubt of two guns near where the ferry steamboat for the Island of Orleans now lands its passengers getting off at St. Joseph.   And Wolfe's third camp was on the height of land to the east of the chute of the Montmorency Falls, with a redoubt of four guns near what is now the eastern end of the railway bridge beyond the Montmorency Cotton Mills.   From the St. Joseph camp, a section of Monckton's brigade was ordered to take up a position on Levis heights opposite the city, where they proceeded to establish the batteries that made such havoc on the buildings of lower town, and even on the edifices in the vicinity of the Grande Place, or what is now known as the Place d'Armes. (See General Introduction).

9. *"To watch Montcalm's defence."*   The line of Montcalm's defence extended all the way from the Montmorency River along the line of the Beauport Flats, and across the St. Charles River, to the two main batteries of the city, a distance of nearly nine miles. (See General Introduction).

10. *"The fleet makes sure its soundings."*   The preliminary survey along the Beauport shore was conducted by Sailing-Master James Cook.   He had scarcely completed his soundings when he was set upon by certain Indians in their canoes.   While escaping from his pursuers, he had just time to leap from the prow of his own smaller boat into a larger one manned by the marines from the *Mercury*, the former craft finally falling into the hands of the Indians.   The presence of the British fleet in the harbour was the embodiment of imminent disaster to the defenders.   The guns of the fleet were gradually reducing the city to a heap of ruins. At length the somewhat fatuous suggestion was made—some say by the profligate Bigot—that a flotilla of fire-ships should be sent amongst Saunders's war-sloops, as they lay at anchorage between the city and the Island of Orleans.   The suggestion, whoever made it, was carried out, though nothing came of it save its being laughed at by the invaders on the land and the water as well, as

something more spectacular than effective—involving an expenditure which might have been spent more judiciously, considering Montcalm's necessities. In the morning all that was left of the fireships comprised a number of charred and smoking hulks, some of which were towed ashore by the British fleetsmen to be out of their way. No harm befell any of the invader's ships from the ill-considered strategy.

11. *"And long he scans the outlet-ford."* So shallow are the waters of the Montmorency as it enters the St. Lawrence that some people have maintained that there must be an underground current by which the unfathomable pit at the base of the cataract empties its contents. As has been said, Wolfe was confident of success from the very first, if he could only force his adversary into the open field, the army of Montcalm with its many incoherences being no match against the trained troops of his own army. The space on which the Montmorency Mills now stand, as may be seen by any one, is altogether too narrow for a general engagement between two armies of the size of the armies in question; and, if the impetuosity of the Grenadiers had to share largely the blame for the subsequent result, the military advice, which led to the assault, can hardly miss being called in question.

12. *"From upper-ford to strand."* There is no more interesting trip for one to take while studying the historical topography of Montmorency than a walk through the woods along its eastern bank from its "outlet-ford" to the "upper-ford" near the lake-like expansion of the river known as DeSable. Every foot of the ground must have been known to Townshend and his subalterns, though where the British redoubts were located it is now impossible to say. There must have been one near where the pillars of the old Suspension Bridge still stand, as if to guard the highway that runs to Ange Gardien; another near the rapids about a mile further up; and a fourth at DeSable.

13. *"And Townshend in command."* A late attempt has been made by a descendant of the Marquis of Townshend to give him the very highest measure of praise for the share he took in the Siege of 1759. No word of praise can be considered too high for the co-operation of this distinguished soldier in the general plan

of the campaign.   He was wise to suggest and faithful to obey, assuming the command as if it were his own, while his superior officer was wrestling with disease and despondency in a peasant's cot beyond his military camping ground.   The brilliancy of General Townshend's soldiership should never, however, be advanced as a discounting of General Wolfe's skill or courage as a commander. The bravery of both cannot be disputed, no more than can be the bravery of Brigadier-Generals Monckton and Murray, who were Townshend's military co-adjutors.

14. *"To the channel or Ange Gardien."*   Some claim that Townshend's division had a reserve at Ange Gardien, the nearest village to the east of the Montmorency, but there is no reliable corroboration of the statement.   It is natural to think, however, that had he been driven from his vantage-ground on the Montmorency heights, he would have retreated eastward along the highway which then led, as it does now, to Ange Gardien and Chateau Richer.

15. *"The singing of the centuries."*   The approaches to the Montmorency Falls have been, in these later years, greatly improved in behalf of the sight-seer—improvements which in no way mar the natural beauty and grandeur of the picturesque, as is so often the case when modernism gets hold of a bit of the beautiful to make money out of it.   Standing by the brink of one of the side precipices, from which can be viewed the "milk-giver" in the fullest majesty of its proportions, the picture is true of it as:

> The rhyming rhythm of the river's mouth,
> Voicing the silence of the centuries:
> A feathery, flaking fleece,
> That fans the landscape's face
> And wreathes with crescent mist
> The rainbowed chasm underneath.

16. *"Repentigny daring Townshend."*   Chevalier De Lévis was in charge of operations at the left extremity of Montcalm's line of defence, and Repentigny seems to have had divisional charge of Montcalm's outposts along the western bank of the Montmorency, subject, of course, to De Lévis' orders.

17. *"The Centurion issuing challenge."* The *Centurion* was one of the most noted of Admiral Saunders's ships, having been the flagship of Commodore Anson, who had sailed round the world in her, before he retired from active service to become First Lord of the Admiralty. Its armament comprised sixty guns, its position during the onset at Montmorency being in mid-channel, between the Island of Orleans and the mouth of that river. It was accompanied by two smaller vessels to cover the immediate landing of the British troops in their barges.

18. *"The Grenadiers advance."* The Grenadiers received their name from being armed with grenades, or hand-shells, to be thrown among the enemy. They were usually expected to be in readiness to take up their position in the van of the attacking army. The men who made the mistake at Montmorency were restored to favour when they were called upon to follow Wolfe in person, as he marched in advance of his right wing on the Plains of Abraham.

19. *"Even under Monckton's eye."* Monckton's troops were being landed with Murray's in perfect order, when the Grenadiers and the Royal Americans were making their advance upon the nearest redoubts of the French army, only to be driven back in disorder.

20. *"The rain weaves shredded pall."* A young officer in the Canadian army, during the North-West Rebellion, undertook one morning to reconnoitre with an umbrella over his head. The derisive shouts of his comrades he is said never to have forgotten. On this occasion at Montmorency, the rain came down in slanting torrents, making the footing dangerously slippery and drenching arms and ammunition till they were all but worthless for the moment. The General in his report says: "A storm came on, and the tide began to make, so that I thought it most advisable not to persevere in so difficult a task."

21. *"The Royals and the Grenadiers."* The former were known as the Royal Americans after they had won renown in many of the contests during the colonial wars, much as had the Royal Rousillons on the French side.

22. *"From impulsiveness and pique."* It is said that but for some misunderstanding between Repentigny and De Lévis on the day of the repulse at Montmorency, the French would have crossed the river up near DeSable to come into close attack with the English detachment left to guard the upper ford; and that had they done so, the English would have been surprised and surrounded in their retreat into the woods, with no possibility of escape. There may be ground for the statement, as far as the friction between the two French commanders is concerned; but there is none for the inference, since any attack of the kind referred to, would only have given Wolfe a chance of meeting his opponents face to face sooner than he did on the Plains of Abraham, in terms of his openly expressed desire for a general engagement in the open.

WOLFE'S MONUMENT

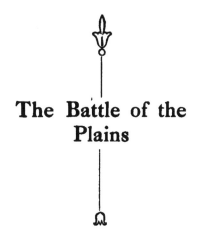

The Battle of the Plains

THE SECOND CONTEST

Introduction to Second Contest

WHILE passing from the city end of the Dufferin Terrace to its extension under the outer wall of the Citadel, the visitor-student is more or less seized with the desire to identify the modern landmarks along the Levis side of the river, from the church of St. Joseph to the church of St. Romuald or New Liverpool. The more prominent of these are the several church edifices, the Levis College, and the Convents. The landmarks of the times immediately before and after the Siege of 1759 can only be approximately located, the overgrowth of modern improvements having obliterated nearly every trace of them. The three forts behind Levis, plainly discernible from the Terrace, were not in existence at the time of that siege, nor for seventy years after, these having been built supplementary to the renewal of the Citadel and the city walls under the advice of the Duke of Wellington, in 1823-32. Wolfe's main battery, which all but destroyed the lower town, was erected not far from the height of land that is now reached by the passenger elevator on the Levis side. The road from St. Nicholas, which now forms part of the main street of the village of Lauzon, was the highway utilized by Wolfe in his operations on that side. Brigadier-General Monckton's camp was situated immediately to the

rear of what is now the site of St. Joseph's Church,
near the ground which is now used as a periodical
camping ground for the Canadian Militia and a target
range. Below the church and on the tongue of land
on which has been excavated the Princess Louise Dry
Dock, there were three redoubts and four small batteries; while on the slopes directly opposite the lower
town there were four redoubts and six batteries, all in
charge of Colonel Burton. These were the batteries
which eventually made it possible for part of the British
fleet in command of Admiral Holmes, under cover of
their guns, to run the gauntlet of the batteries of the
beleaguered city. And, standing over the blending of
the old and the new architectural groupings of buildings in lower town, the student of events may pause
for a moment to make note of what had been happening on the sites beneath and behind his stand-point,
before Wolfe and his associates had finally made up
their minds to take full advantage of the mistake the
besieged had made in not fortifying the Levis side of
the river as they had the Beauport side.

The persistent violence from the Levis land batteries and those of the fleet had virtually left no house
in lower town tenantable. The little chapel of Notre
Dame des Victoires, whose spire and façade still form
the most interesting of the ancient landmarks of lower
town, had nothing left of it save its walls, which were
pieced out in its re-erection as soon as the siege was
over, much as they are to be seen to-day. The streets
were impassable, as after an earthquake or devastating
fire, with the debris of overthrown buildings obstruct-
ing them and rendering unserviceable many of the
smaller batteries on the slopes and by the river side.

The chapels of the Recollets and the Jesuits, as well as the Seminaries, were in ruins; and so widely sweeping had raged the storm of shot and shell from the ships, that the district known as the "Palais" in the vicinity of Palace Gate, even to the Intendant's Palace, was all but wiped out. The establishments of the Ursulines and the Hospitalières had to be vacated by their pious-minded inmates; indeed, the condition of things indicated that, if the invader eventually should take the place, it would be hardly worth the taking, as far as property values were concerned. Nay, what had escaped the bombardment, had more or less fallen a prey to the bands of pillagers who, it seems, may always be looked for during any calamity of this sort.

Nor had the bombardment brought any immediate advantages to the besiegers, as long as Wolfe kept wrestling with the great main issue of driving Montcalm from behind his Beauport safeguards, unless it was the incidental opening up of a waterway past the city batteries. As one of the side cruelties then sanctioned by war, it was in keeping with the ruthlessness of the corps of rangers and light infantry that these ravagers were let loose against the country parishes, with seemingly no other end in view save the destruction of private property. Even when Admiral Holmes had succeeded in anchoring part of his division of the fleet above the city, there was nothing further for his ships to do in the meantime, since any effective bombardment from that direction was out of the question. Indeed, it was not until Montcalm had sent Bougainville to Cap Rouge with a strong detachment, that incidents occurring up the river beyond Cape Diamond entered into the general event of the siege.

And it is from the end of the Terrace beyond the walls of the Citadel, that the lesson of the movements on the river above may best be learned, up to the time when Wolfe, with his full army under his immediate command, came drifting down with the tide towards the inlet or cove this side of the Sillery Church.

In the Levis woods, on the near side of the Etcbemin River, fifteen hundred soldiers, Indians, and volunteers, some of the latter being students of the Laval Seminary, set out one dark night to silence the batteries in charge of Colonel Burton, by picking off the gunners in a flank attack of musketry. They had gone across from Sillery; and, girding themselves for the march through the woods, they secured their boats on the beach in such a way as to have them instantly ready, should they be surprised before accomplishing their design. They never reached the guns of Burton's batteries. The pitchy darkness and their own fears seem to have turned their heads, as they passed from thicket to thicket; and, at last, the confusion became such that they began to fire on one another, bringing on a panic that sent them in headlong haste back to their boats. The escape was the occasion of not a little satirical merriment in both armies, the incident being nicknamed the ''Scholars' Battle.''

When General Murray was sent with twelve hundred men up the river to attempt a crossing somewhere above Cap Rouge, he was more than once hindered in his operations by mixed troops of Indians and French rangers; but none of these interruptions attained to the dignity of being called a battle. And so closely was Bougainville on the lookout for Murray,

that on two several occasions the latter was prevented
from landing near Pointe-aux-Trembles. Murray's main
achievement up-river was when he effected a landing
at Deschambault, where a large quantity of loot fell
into his hands, besides the information from inter-
cepted despatches that General Amherst had been
meeting with crowning success in the west, and might
be looked for at Quebec as soon as he had tried conclusions with Bourlamaque on the Richelieu River.

Murray's seizure at Deschambault seems to have
given heart to other excursions, having for their object
the pouncing upon the supplies of provisions and
ammunition that were being carried into Quebec from
week to week. And these excursions, and the presence
of Holmes's vessels to implement them with the necessary river craft, could not but lead Montcalm to suspect
that his policy of a close defence behind his Beauport
lines was no lasting policy for the saving of the city
itself. There were few military projects or suggestions
over which the French governor and the French general could agree, without some show of friction between
them personally. Montcalm had been solicitous from
the beginning about the defenceless state of the city
in its rear. But, for the sake of peace, the hero of
Carillon had given way to the petulant governor in
the matter of strengthening the approaches to the
Plains of Abraham. Vaudreuil was at first sure that
no fleet would think of daring the dangers of the narrows overlooked by the city's batteries. And it was
not until Holmes had taken his ships through these
narrows that he became as anxious as Montcalm to
have every cove and headland protected, from Cap
Rouge to Sillery, and had even a redoubt built at the

head of the steep up which Wolfe was finally to ascend
to the levels of the plateau.

At last the British army was on the move towards
the south banks of the St. Lawrence. Montcalm
made no attempt to interrupt the movements from
Montmorency on the part of Townshend to the Island
of Orleans, nor even when he saw the troops of Murray and Townshend on their way to join Monckton's
brigade on the grounds behind what is now the site
of the St. Joseph Church.

The camp on the Island was left in charge of Major
Guy Carleton, who took good care to make the reserve
left in his hands as formidable looking as possible,
by parading them in recurring relays before the eyes
of the enemy at Beauport. The three Brigadier-
Generals, Monckton, Townshend, and Murray, were
all of one mind with General Wolfe in the change of
plan, and were all equally active in getting their brigades up the river to a point where they might be taken
on board of Holmes's ships and the boats attached
to them. Descending from the high banks of Levis,
the English regiments, as they were crossing the Etcbemin River where Murray had met with opposition on
his way up the St. Lawrence, became exposed to the
firing from one of Vaudreuil's batteries near Sillery.
Near where the piers of the Quebec Bridge now overlook the outlet of the Chaudière, these troops were
taken on board the ships that were in waiting for them
there, with a large number of flat-bottomed barges
under towage for their accommodation. The eyes
of the French outposts on the other side of the river
must have kept marvelling at the flotilla on its way
up with the tide, their commanders being no doubt

unable to make out what the procession all meant, and being puzzled all the more when the tide brought some of the boats back again. As the tide bore part of the flotilla back down the river again, several feints were made by the British at landing, in face of the enemy's fire, Wolfe being again in supreme command, with seemingly recovered health, as the squadron kept up its manœuvres from one trip to another on the turn of the tide. No word had escaped the General up to the day before the battle, that could be taken to indicate where he intended to make a final landing. The French from their outposts became more and more bewildered over the hesitancy of the besiegers. For over a week the mystification continued; while daily reports were being carried to Montcalm at Beauport of the make-believe encounters that were taking place along the northern shore of the river, with no injury to the outposts; and he no doubt came to think that his adversary was as badly off for a landing place then, as he had been when making his attempt at Montmorency. And this is how the manœuvring was kept up, according to what Dr. Miles says in his *French Régime:*

"Whenever the vessels came to anchor opposite places on the bank, which seemed to be favourable for disembarking, and when the barges full of men showed themselves, the detachments on shore would form in line on the commanding heights; the horse would then dismount, and while their field-pieces were discharged, expending ammunition to no purpose, the whole would run down the steeper bank, with loud shouts towards their lower defences. On the water the English soldiers would remain silent and attentive in their boats, unmindful of the noisy demonstrations on the shore, reserving their fire for the word of command, and waiting in patience to see whether or not it was the real intention of their officers to attempt a landing."

Two days before the memorable thirteenth of the month arrived, the soldiers in Wolfe's army, men and officers, were informed that all this manœuvring was at last to come to an end. Montcalm stubbornly remained at Beauport, and Bougainville seldom left the vicinity of Cap Rouge. The French army was thus to some extent a divided army. Every man on the British side was given to understand that the main event of a pitched battle was at hand. They were now to be ready for something more than the feints which had been amusing them for a week back. It was not necessary, they were told, for everyone to know where the actual landing was to take place: the first fine night would reveal that in time, with everybody ready to follow to the letter their instructions.

And these were the final instructions issued on the day before the thirteenth:

"A corps will be left to secure the landing place, while the rest march on to bring the French and Canadians to battle. The officers and men will recollect what their country expects of them, and what a determined body of soldiers inured to war is capable of doing, against five weak French battalions of regulars, mingled with a disorderly peasantry. The soldiers must be attentive and obedient to their officers, and resolute in the execution of their duty."

At length the whole of Wolfe's up-river forces were afloat, the detachments set ashore at St. Nicholas having all been taken on board during the two days preceding the battle. It was understood that on the evening of the twelfth there should be a cannonading of the Beauport lines by the fleet, innocuous as it might be, and an even more incessant bombardment of the city than usual, from the batteries in Levis, so that the attention of the defenders in front should not be attracted towards what was happening in the rear of the city, as something different to what had been happening for nearly eight days before, namely, the floating of the enemy's ships up and down the river at the will of the tide. At ten o'clock the night before the momentous day, the tide had carried the ships of the line, with their subsidiary craft of flat-bottomed barges, to a point on the river nearly opposite the heights where Bougainville had his central outlook; and when the tide had turned, the procession of floating, shadowy shapes began to pass slowly and silently down towards Sillery and the baylet or cove of which the Sillery Church now stands a prominent landmark, as we look up the river towards it from the end of the extension of the Dufferin Terrace.

A usual question is asked at this point in nearly every narrative that has been written of this wondrous tidal voyage: Why was the British flotilla not interrupted in its course by the detachments and outposts of the French stationed along the river? There were interruptions, and some of the soldiers and sailors on the fleet and in the barges were killed and wounded on the way to and fro. The gliding past of the fleet came to be no new thing to those on the outlook for it. Besides, each detachment had its own outpost to hold by, irrespective of what the issue of any of the feints at fighting might be. The duties of the one outpost seemed to be fulfilled when the fleet had once passed within the venue of the next outpost. In a word, the procession of the British up and down with the tide had become something of a daily occurrence, and the French outposts having become used to the occurrence, were caught thinking less about it than they ought to have done, on the morning of the thirteenth. A week's manœuvring with the tide, as Wolfe expected, had thrown the defenders out of their reckoning: the wily General had lulled his opponents out of their keen-edged anxiety.

The story continues to be repeated that when the tide had carried the advance barges round the headland of Sillery towards the head of the *Anse au Foulon*, a challenge came from the heights above, in the query, *"Qui vive?"*

And the answer is said to have been returned by an officer of the Fraser Highlanders, who, we are told, had learned French while serving as a soldier in Flanders, and whom a writer has sought to identify with Colonel Nairne; the first seigneur of Murray Bay—the answer having been: *"La France."*

"A quel regiment?" is said to have come as a second query, and *"De la reine"* is further said to have been the Highlander's reply, who, it is further stated, in order to disarm all suspicion, asked his questioner not to make any noise, since the vessels were only carrying provisions to the city.

"Ne faites pas bruit, ces sont les vivres!"

The phrase "these are the provisions" has given rise to the conjecture that such a deception had been practised on more than one of the outposts on the

way down, whereas the truth of the matter is that
the English ships and their outfit of barges were so
well known to the French outposts that no such deception as is represented in the above anecdote could
have been practised on them. In fact the Colonel
Nairne story has to be taken as having something of
the myth about it. (See Note 11.)

And the manner of the ascent proves it. There
was no one abroad on the slope leading up to Verger's
outpost to put such a query. Before any attempt
had been made to climb the pathway up from the cove,
or any noise of any kind had been made, the General
had taken the precaution to send an advance of Highlanders further down than the head of the *Anse au
Foulon*, there to make a first escalade of the steep
bank, with an after movement on the unlucky Verger,
all unprepared for such a surprise. So difficult of
ascent had this place seemed to Vaudreuil's scouts,
that no guard had been provided for, at least no guard
was met with by the intrepid Scotsmen as they emerged
from their perilous climb, to take breath on the level
ground above. The nearest outpost, namely that in
command of a certain Captain Verger, who had not
brought a very good name for vigilance from Acadia
with him, when he happened to meet with favour from
Governor Vaudreuil, was situated but a few hundred
yards to the west, immediately overlooking the partially blocked trail or pathway up which the English
army had to be led on the way to the plateau above.
The Highlanders were not long in arriving at Verger's
outpost, putting his soldiers to flight, and capturing
the heedless commander himself, whom it is said they
found asleep in his tent. Immediately the message

was sent to those in charge on the beach that the coast
was clear, as far as the French outpost at the edge
of the slope was concerned, thus giving a first apprisal
for a general disembarkation from the transports and
barges at anchorage in the waters of the bay or cove.
The dawn was not fully come when the British army
was ready for its march towards the final scene of the
conflict.

. .   .   .

The battlefield of the Plains of Abraham may be
most readily reached from the city end of the Dufferin Terrace, in a direct line east and west, by way
of St. Louis Street and Grande Allée, and thence out
to the St. Louis Road. The impression that the open
space at the southern end of Maple Avenue, and extending thence to the cliff, is the battlefield proper,
has all but received its quietus; at least, the visitor
should at once dismiss such an idea, should it be urged
in his or her hearing. Until very recently, that particular space of ground, now part of the Battlefields
Park, was had in use for military reviews and kindred
outdoor recreations; and the citizens, on their way
out to witness such exhibitions, came to acquire the
habit of asking one another by way of greeting: "Are
you going out to the Plains to-day?" or some other
such a query, in which the term "the Plains" came
to have a narrowed connotation. The famous battlefield, that witnessed the Battle of the Plains as well
as the Battle of Sainte-Foye, in reality extends from
the Belvedere Road and the Wolfe's Cove Road, and
beyond them to the Buttes-à-Neveu, or Perrault's
Hill, where stands to-day the spacious Franciscan
Chapel and Nunnery. This latter is the highest point

of the Grande Allée—the highest point in Quebec, in
fact—and it is from the crest of this slope, extending
north and south in a line with what is now Claire Fontaine Street, that the troops of Montcalm, with the
General himself standing at their centre a hundred
yards or so from what is now the site of the Francis-
cans' property, first could count the full muster of the
British battalions.   These battalions were marshalled
on the level ground that extended in a line running
north and south, and parallel with the line of Montcalm's army, from what is now the junction of Maple
Avenue with St. Louis Road.   As it was from the
centre of his army that Wolfe at first issued his orders
to his two wings, the two rival generals must have
been standing all but *vis-a-vis* to each other, before
the marching began towards mid-field.   Neither the
old Citadel nor any of its outworks were to be seen
from the position taken up by Wolfe, these being
hidden behind the slopes on which the French army
was marshalled, and even Montcalm's left wing was
visible only in part, notably the companies that held
the ground in the hollow between the Buttes-à-Neveu
and the rising ground on which the jail buildings were
afterwards erected.   According to the express orders
of Wolfe, this latter rising ground was taken possession of by the Louisbourg Grenadiers, whose ranks
had been so disastrously decimated at Montmorency;
and it is from it, perhaps, that the plan of the battle
may be most advantageously examined.

Looking northward in the direction of the irregular
outlines of the Laurentides and the valley of the St.
Charles, the surveyor of the site of the battle has on his
right the spreading suburbs and the city proper lying

beyond and enclosed within its walls; on his left, Wolfe's Cove, known at the time of the battle as *Anse au Foulon*, and now indicated at its entrance by the spire of Sillery Church; and behind him the waters of the majestic St. Lawrence.

When the news was spread abroad that the British had at last gained a footing on the plateau behind the city, Montcalm was as yet with his army at Beauport.

"They have discovered our weakest point of defence after all!" he is reported to have exclaimed, when the tidings was carried to him across the bridge of boats.

For nearly three months he had succeeded in keeping his adversary at bay; and when Wolfe, as a last resort before it was too late, followed Holmes's division of the fleet as it kept on the move between Pointe-aux-Trembles and Sillery, Montcalm had provided against the suspicious movement by sending Bougainville to Cap Rouge with a detachment of two thousand or more, on the understanding that the north bank of the river would be guarded as the Beauport shore had been, if not so strongly. As has been said, there were outposts located all along this bank; and, relying on these, Montcalm's anxiety was, in a measure, set at rest for the moment. The alarming news was therefore as unexpected to him, perhaps, as they were to Vaudreuil, who had been busying himself over these outposts up the river. Montcalm is said to have ridden in great haste to verify the news in person, before he undertook to change his plans for the protection of the Beauport approaches to the city. Possibly on that memorable ride, between five and six in the morning, he gave his first instructions for immediate concentration towards Ringfield and the bridge of boats; we know at least that by ten o'clock his army had reached the open spaces beyond the walls by way of St. John Gate and St. Louis Gate, ready to be drawn up in battle array along the Buttes-à-Neveu.

The two armies were not long in sight of each other until the work in hand was inaugurated by certain skirmishers lurking in the woods of the Ste. Foye Road. Montcalm had charge of the centre of his battle-line, that centre including the veteran regiment of Languedoc and the battalion of Béarn. The left wing stationed over by the Cove Fields, and comprising the regiments of Guienne, the Royal Rousillons, and the Militia of Three Rivers, was in charge of M. de Sénézergues. The right wing, spread out from the line of John Street, and including the battalion of La Sarre and the Militia of Quebec and Montreal, was in the hands of M. St. Ours.

On the British side, the centre, which comprised the regiments of Lascelles, Anstruther, and the Fraser Highlanders, was under the sub-command of Brigadier-General Murray. The right wing, extending towards the grouping of the Louisbourg Grenadiers near the jail-site, and including the regiments of Bragg, Otway, and Kennedy, was in charge of Brigadier-General Monckton. Possibly, to restrain the impetuosity of the Grenadiers, which had led to such disaster at Montmorency, Wolfe himself, as Commander-in-chief, took up his position in front of these, to the right of Monckton. The left wing was under the direction of Brigadier-General Townshend, including as it did the Amherst regiment and the Light Infantry, with a reserve of the Royal Americans in its rear under the command of Colonel Burton.

A first effort in the contest on the part of the defenders was to harass the outer companies of Townshend's wing by a skirmishing fire from certain Canadian and Indian sharpshooters in ambush along the Ste. Foye Road. Townshend ordered a side attack by one or two of his companies, the main division moving forward with the centre and the left wing, as soon as Wolfe had given the word of command for the whole British line to advance against the moving columns of Montcalm.

The contest was one of very short duration, when once the contesting lines came together in the final shock. There is even a present-day excitement from the mind-picture one may make of the rush of the French from their outlook on the Buttes-à-Neveu, with two of their columns hurrying towards the left, and one towards the right, keeping up a constant firing as they approached what is now the line of De Salaberry Street. Nor was that rush interrupted by any firing from the red-coats, until the French had come up to within forty or fifty yards of them; for the order had gone forward that not a British musket was to be fired until the contestants should be able to see "the whites of one another's eyes."

The first shock of the battle must have taken place four hundred yards or so east of the lane now called Wolfe's Avenue. Wolfe was leading in person when the first movement forward was made. Then he seems to have joined the Grenadiers as they started from their vantage-ground at the foot of which the monument to the British general now stands. While leading in this second movement, he was wounded first in the wrist and second in the groin, and finally received his death wound near what are now the grounds of the Protestant Home. The hero's monument marks the exact spot where he expired, he having been carried thither for shelter behind the grassy slope, and beyond the rush of the British onset against the wavering lines of the French. There was a thicket near by where the old cemetery of De Salaberry Street is now enclosed as part of the grounds of the St. Bridget Asylum; and the fact that this formed a partial shelter for some of Montcalm's skirmishers, before the battle began and after the rout started, leads to the conclusion that the final shock took place along what is now the line of De Salaberry Street, or a little to the west of it—a stretch of ground well within sight of those standing near the dying commander, when they exclaimed in his hearing that the opposing army was in full flight.

One can hardly realize how quickly retreat and pursuit started after that second shock. As Sir Gilbert Parker describes it in three of his pithy sentences:

"When the French were within forty yards, Wolfe raised his sword, a command rang down the long line of battle, and, with a crash of one terrible cannon-shot, the British muskets sang out together. After the smoke had cleared a little, another volley followed with almost the same precision. A little breeze lifted the smoke and mist, and a wayward sunlight showed Montcalm's army retreating like a long white wave from a rocky shore."

The Battle of the Plains

WHILE the centuries were meeting, with their bur-
    dens of renown,
The city round Cape Diamond,[1] sitting queen on
    rock-built throne,
Received, with gratulation, the *famæ* that they
    brought,
To swell the annals of her past with intuitions
    fraught,
With the tumult of her darkest days, shedding
    lustre on her pride,
As the nations vied to share the *fête*[2] the centuries
    purveyed.

And her darkest day, perchance, was that wherein
    she was beset,
By the might of Britain proud arrayed New France
    to subjugate;
And the marvel grows, as we read the tale, how a
    golden dawn arose
From the darkness of that day of strife, still smil-
    ing, as it glows—
Yea, smiling on our peace of days, the glory of a
    realm,
Where brotherhood restrains the hand that peace
    would overwhelm.

67

There was lifting of that darkness, in the days
    before the dawn,
When the news first reached the city that the Brit-
    ish had withdrawn
From the beach at Montmorency, under stress of
    hope deferred,
Perchance awhile to ponder as to who it was had erred:
" 'Tis like they've struck a problem" as 'twas
    rumoured in the town,
"That may stagger Admiral Saunders' and make
    the General frown."

Yea, a problem 'twas whose solving might well
    enhance alarm,
With the lower town in ruins and the country all
    a-storm,
From Pointe-aux-Trembles to Bout de l'Isle,' and
    spreading further south,
Where the smoking homesteads ravaged lay, beyond
    the Chaudière's mouth;'
Yea, a problem whose most stubborn phase of at-
    tack against defence
Leaves the Beauport line unbroken and all landing
    still a chance.   .

"Out in the open," Wolfe had said, "the defenders
    must be drawn,
"If we would take the city before the summer's gone."
"Behind our lines," Montcalm had said, "there's
    victory in delay,
"Till winter drives them from our coasts in hap-
    less disarray."
And old Dame Nature seemed to hold the toss of
    how 'twould be,
With no loophole to the heights above to ward the
    invader's key.'

The fleet has run the gauntlet[7] of the city's hottest fire,
And the problem still finds Nature slow to imple-
    ment desire:
"We must bide our time for longer, in this game of
    do or die,
"With our courage kept in training, under our
    General's eye:
"While our frigates and their barges float hither
    and again,
"His thoughts are all of victory, to the masking
    of his pain."[8]

For, in truth the ships kept swinging, like a pen-
    dulum, with the tide,
From beyond Cap Rouge to Sillery,[9] while Bougain-
    ville would chide,[10]
From his shifting musters near the shore, with
    shell and musketry,
While Verger kept his outlook watch[11] against
    calamity,
Beyond the Samos battery,[12] high on his vantage-
    ground,
Against approach to the plains above where vic-
    tory might be found.

And all the while the Beauport camp had woes its
    own to bear,
From a hovering in the harbour and desertion in
    the rear:
With no De Lévis nigh at hand[13] nor Bourlamaque
    the bold,[14]
Only Vaudreuil discordant[15] with his counsels manifold:
Yea, the bitterness for Montcalm[16] grew keener
    every day,
When he saw war's venue widen out, to counteract
    delay.

At length the fateful night drew near, with espion-
   age awake,
Foe watching foe with quickened eye, ascendancy
   at stake;
The tide the only neutral, and constant in its swing,
To the foe upon its waters and the foe in covering;
And evermore the brave Wolfe watched, conceal-
   ing every pain
That shot within his feebling frame, as he com-
   passed out his plan.

At length the fateful night arrived, starlit and
   breathing quiet,
And the armament made floating pause, as mid-
   night took its flight:
"The tide has turned," the outlook cries, as he
   notes Cap Rouge ahead,
Whence Bougainville, from day to day, his skirmishers had led,
In contingents to the waterside, to obviate ascent,
Keeping surprise at elbow's length, to anticipate
   lament.

Yea, the tide has turned more ways than one, and
   the main-top lights repeat
The message for a moment, as a signal to the fleet:
Then the barges steering townward drift, without
   the sound of oar,
The silence all the deeper when broken by the roar
From the Levis forts and Saunders' ships storming
   the battered town,
As if nothing else were happening to alarm ap-
   proaching dawn.

And who is there who has not heard of the stam-
   pede up the steep,

When once poor Verger was surprised with his sen-
    tinels asleep:
How a British force, five thousand strong,[17] soon
    spread in proud array,
To challenge entrance to the town in terms of Brit-
    ish sway;
Nay, who has failed to prize aright the burden of
    renown
The centuries bring to glorify the pride that is our
    own?

O Fate! whose shadows flit within the pale
Of memory's maze as, seeming near, the wail
Of heroes' hopes, spent in the rage of war,
Brings echo from the past a-seeming far!
How pause we on the verge of instant joy,
To scan the pride and woe of life's alloy
Inwove on history's page—the tale of fate
And ecstasy sublimed by tribal hate!
Athwart these plains, where armies erst have fought
In short-timed strife, we still would wing in thought,
To read heroic day-dream in the alarm
Of nearing clouds arrayed for battle-storm—
To watch the flash that livid gleams on death,
While peals its thunder o'er the torrid heath.
Is that the pibroch of the Celtic braves[18]
That calls contending kinsmen to their graves?
Are these the shouts of liberty that bid
A budding nation vaunt its new-born pride?
Adown the hollow there may still be found,
Near by an obscure pillar, helmet-crowned,
The spot revered,[19] where Wolfe victorious fell,
Precedent to his rival's dying knell:
'Twas yonder near the slope, in full array,
While yet the scene was one of instant fray,

He saw, through haze of death, his trusty Celt
Rush at the foe: 'twas here his great heart felt
At once the greatest mortal joy and pain,
Elate with victory as he passed within.

   .   .   .   .   .

  Abreast the lines the hero fell,
    In the thickest of the fray,
  And he whispered near him not to tell
    Till victory crowned the day.
  As he lay upon the greensward slope,
    With the sunlight in his eyes,
  His soul still bounded, winged with hope,
    To grasp ambition's prize.

  A soldier trained, when his king he served,
    His courage never paled:
  Against his feeble body nerved,
    His spirit never failed.
  If he felt his race its goal had found,
    For him 'twas glory's gain,
  In the hopes that still dared hover round
    His battlefield of pain.

  A moment's thought for those he loved
    In the dear old English home,
  And then again his longings roved
    To sift the cannon's boom:[20]
  Will he die before the victory
    Assured is in his ears,
  To sound the valedictory
    Of his earthly hopes and fears?

  Ah, no, for stands a messenger,[21]
    With tidings from the plain,
  Whose troubled smile is harbinger
    Of joy repressed by pain;

For he sees his General's dying fast,
   Whate'er the news he bears,
And his heart, with sadness overcast,
   His zeal restrains with tears.

Yet stooping o'er the prostrate form,
   To catch the hero's eye,
He tells how, fast before the storm,
   They run the musketry:
"Who run?" the dying General said,
   Though no fear was in his face,
For of nothing was he e'er afraid,
   Unless it were disgrace:

Besides he knew his men were brave,
   Tried veterans in the field—
From Louisbourg victorious wave,[22]
   That seldom thought to yield:
And when the soldier knelt to tell
   How the foe it was that ran,
"So soon!" was all that feebly fell
   From the lips resisting pain.

"Send Burton,"[23] and he breathed again,
   "To check them in retreat,
"To guard St. Charles's bridge and plain,[24]
   "And make secure defeat."
Alas! 'twas duty's last behest,
   In faintest whisper sighed,
For death his soldier-victim pressed
   And would not be defied.

But now to him death had no sting,
   Though his years had been but brief,
For he knew his deeds would joyous ring,[25]
   To soothe a mother's grief.

"Now God be praised," his last words came,
  "For happy do I die";
And those around him knew his fame
  Was immortality.

And still the centuries love to tell
  Of victory's glorious sheen,
That gilds the plain whereon he fell,
  To keep his glory green;
For his renown is Britain's might,
  That finds her own the fame
Of those who death have dared in fight
  For the honour of her name.

.   .   .   .   .   .

With speed of light, as on the silvered plate
Of photographic art, the tints innate
On fancy's film, begrimed with battle-breath,
Make memory-wreathings round the hero's death.
Across the gorse-clad plain, in dawn's faint light,
We still would scan the prelude of the fight,
And breathless watch the panoramic view
Of proud array on war's broad avenue.
See, how the invader's musters press the edge
Of slopes worn headlong near the river's sedge!
With like defence along the yonder side,
Behold the left wing, steeled with veteran pride,
Fringing the field, defiant of defeat,
Howe'er the strife may test them with its heat.
From the woods, afar and near, a galling fire
Gives instant signal that the foe's astir;
Yea, see the dust clouds climbing up the air,
As Montcalm brings his hastening cohorts near—
A band to muster on the invader's flank
His thousands, hurried-lined from rank to rank,
Instant for onset, wing to wing devised,
Foe facing foe at last, all undisguised!

Lo, first, Sainte-Foye gives tongue across the plain,[26]
And hails disaster in its fringe of slain!
Though Townshend and his men, with speed of
    wind,
A needed aid for comrades instant find,
While still the General's urgent voice rings out,
To re-assure his men with valour's shout.

.   .   ..

And now we see, as fancy's freaks approve,
In lights phantasmic, French and British move,
To meet in middle shock, not far afield,
Where bravery o'ercome by skill must yield.
All heedless of the stolid stern advance
Of kilted silence giving countenance
To mandate, soon the French the strife begin,
Rushing pell-mell to meet disaster's din.
Their fitful volleys on the British lines
But mark the wounds which marching courage
    tines,
By filling up the gaps, at duty's call,
By daring death's demands as comrades fall.
Alas, the havoc! Yet, all-skilful led,
The British cohorts time no timid tread,
Nor fire a shot, howe'er their wills rebel,
Till, at command, their every shot can tell;
And, when the word goes forth, the plain is thrilled
By thunderous flash and crash, full death-distilled,
To time its poison in one musket roll,
Against the faith that flouts its own control.

.   .   .

What strange *eclat* to us that volley brings,
As through our souls becalmed it booming rings!
We hear its echoes through the aisles of time,
And hallow it for us in prose and rhyme,

While yet we hear our wistful dreams reveal
The cheers that still a nation's victory seal.
The reeling rout three waves of fire complete,
Till, o'er the glebe, it 'scapes with hurrying feet,
To throng the turbid streets of old Quebec,
And breathe a moment from the battle's wreck.
'Twas then, with Wolfe and Montcalm stricken
    down,[27]
A failing cause brought Canada renown;
'Twas then, when France o'ercome its task forsook,
The prestige of New France, decaying, broke.

.   .   .

'Twas in the rear the hero fell,
    A victim of defeat,
That weeps to sound a brave man's knell,
    A brave man in retreat;
When he saw his wavering army fly,
    Across the smoke-girt plain,
His great heart heaved a bitter sigh,
    Though his soul defied the pain.

Thére ran confusion like a tide
    At full ebb down the slopes,
As the fragments of a soldier's pride
    Lay shattered with his hopes—
Those hopes, which quickened at the dawn,
    Had brightened with the morn,
Now draggled by defeat and drawn
    Beneath the feet of scorn.

'Tis true his men had braved the storm
    Of British musketry,
As, at his word, they dared re-form,
    Before they turned to flee;

But nothing could a victory urge
   'Gainst lines that never swerved,
Whose front drove back the battle's surge,
   In face of death unnerved.

'Twas as he rode by panic's flank,
   To re-assure retreat,
That, pressed by death's chance bolt, he sank
   At anxious duty's feet;
Yet, stricken down, his only thought
   Was how the tide to stem,
As from his steed he vainly sought
   A lost cause to redeem.

Even when the rout found rest at last
   From the galling musketeers,
His orders issued thick and fast,
   To calm his followers fears:
Though wounded sore, he gave no heed
   To what betokened death,
For he felt his country's plight had need
   Of a patriot's latest breath.

At last, when told his end was near,
   'Twas then he found relief:
" I shall not live, the doom to hear
   " Of a city wrung with grief;
" 'Tis God's hand presses on the town,
   " Perchance He'll set it free,
" Besides, the foe hath high renown
   " That claims the victory."

And when Ramézay sought his couch,[28]
   To urge a last behest,
No tremor throbbed the hero's touch,
   As the soldier's hand he pressed;
6

"To France the fair be ever leal,
  "Whatever may betide,
"Soil not her lilies when you seal
  "A treaty with her pride;

"Our foe is generous as brave,
  "Nor will good faith betray;
"He'll never make New France a slave,
  "Though victor in the fray;
"This night I spend the last on earth,
  "Communing with my God,
"The morning's sun will bring me birth
  "Within His high abode."

"So God be with you all," he said,
  As he chid his comrades' tears,
And turned with pain upon his bed,
  Still unsubdued with fears;
And soon from earth there passed a soul
  As brave as France has seen,
And as the centuries onward roll,
  His fame keeps fresh and green.

                .   .   .   .

And now these slopes this deadly conflict saw,
Awhile becrowned with emblem of the law,[20]
Provides a vantage where the eye may rest
Upon the plateau's windings, crest to crest.
Besmoothed of knolls and kindred grass-grown
      knowes,
Whereon the peaceful kine were wont to browse;
Released at last from secular neglect,
That savoured of an empire's disrespect;
Nor longer desecrate as soul-gifts are,
When fealty's buried in the debonair.

A household word to us in fame and name,
Why may we not enhance its empire fame,
To assure our sharing in an empire's pride,
Children of her who ruleth far and wide?
Ay, sacred place it is, where one may kneel
To bless the peace the joys of time reveal!
Yea, even when the winter's robe in train
Blankets with milk-white warmth the drowsy plain,
We fondly read the lesson of the lea,
That here a blending sleeps of destiny,
Which gifts to us a freedom solemnized,
With what these slopes adorned have symbolized.

.   .   .   .   .   .

And so the centuries, as they meet, with their bur-
    dens of renown,
May greet the good old city, sitting queen on rock-
    built throne,
Making aye their gratulations with the *famæ*[30]
    which they bring,
To swell the annals of the past that to her present
    cling;
And the tumult of her early days will lustre still
    her pride,
When the nations vie to share the *fête* the cen-
    turies have purveyed.

Notes on "The Battle of the Plains"

1. *"The city round Cape Diamond."* This promontory, which is the most easterly escarpment of the plateau extending from Cap Rouge to the Dufferin Terrace, may be looked upon as having the city all around it, since the configuration of which it is the headlong ending divides the city into three parts, namely, the upper town; the lower town with the buildings on Champlain Street for its continuation; and the suburbs of St. Roch and St. Sauveur. Champlain named the great bluff Mont du Gas, in honour of Sieur de Monts' family name. It received its present name from the silicate crystals, or rough diamonds, found in its vicinity. The original name given to the rock by the Indians was *Uapistikaiats*, or white cape, hence the French *Cap Blanc*, which is still given to that part of it which overlooks the Church of Notre Dame de la Garde on Champlain Street.

2. *"As the nations vied to share the fête."* From within the Empire and beyond its bounds, the greatest interest was taken in the celebration of the three hundredth birthday of Canada. And the interest is not likely to slacken, considering the phenomenon of the blending of so many nationalities that is still to be seen in Canada's present day populations, not yet all shorn of their distinctive characteristics.

3. *"That may stagger Admiral Saunders."* Sir Charles Saunders was selected by William Pitt to accompany Wolfe, his competency to fulfil the task of admiral of the British fleet having been tested while serving under Lord Anson. The section of the fleet that was sent out to co-operate with Wolfe in the taking of Quebec, was one of the finest seaworthy armaments Britain could collect, consisting as it did of fifty vessels; and the unanimity

81

that characterized the relationship maintained between admiral and general had certainly much to do with the success of the whole undertaking. Sir Charles was a Scotsman by birth, and came into his reward as a naval officer, the year after the capture of Quebec, as Lieutenant-General of Marines, attaining eventually to the high position of First Lord of the Admiralty. He died full of honours in the year 1775, the year in which Quebec was called upon to face another siege. His associates at Quebec were Admirals Holmes and Durell, the former having been appointed admiral in command of the station at Jamaica the year after the siege of Quebec by Wolfe.

4. *"From Pointe-aux-Trembles to Bout de l'Isle."* The former took its name from the rapids that disturbed the waters of the St. Lawrence near it, before the channel had been cleared of its rocks in later times to facilitate navigation. Bout de l'Isle is the name given to the eastern extremity of the Island of Orleans. Strange to say, both of these names are applied to localities in the vicinity of Montreal.

5. *"Beyond the Chaudière's mouth."* The parishes along the valley of the Chaudière, one of the six largest tributaries of the St. Lawrence, have always been famed for their fertility. The picturesqueness of the localities around the mouth of the river is enhanced by the Chaudière Falls, which before they were robbed of their energy and primeval grandeur in the interest of electrical exploitation, were to be fittingly represented in such a stanza as the following:

> Boiling caldron, seethe and circle,
> Brattling o'er the shredding shale:
> Toil and tumble, roar and rumble, crash and crumble,
> In thy craters water-worn—
> Portent of a thousand ripples,
> Gleaming, glistening far below.

6. *"To ward the invader's key"* means to fit in with his purposes, as a key fits into its ward. There were virtually three possible ascents which Wolfe and his men took advantage of in their climb up from the river's banks to the plains above. One of these was the main path up the steep incline, or *Sentier au Foulon,*

which had been impeded by the defenders by windfalls or trees cut down on purpose. The second, which the few Highlanders climbed, hand over hand, to get back on Verger's outpost, was a few hundred yards down from the Cove towards the city. The third was along the course of the *Ruisseau St. Denis,* or St. Denis Brook, a streamlet which drains the glebe-lands of Wolfesfield and the farm-lands in its vicinity. At the head of the first path, which is now the highway lane leading up to the St. Louis Road, was situated Verger's camp, the remains of which may still be deciphered. Up the St. Denis Brook, it is said that one solitary gun was dragged, all that Wolfe had with him when the battle began, the sailors from the ships afterwards being ordered to wade the stream as they carried on their backs provisions and ammunition from the bateaux below.

7. *"The fleet has run the gauntlet."* The first attempt to take the British ships past the danger point between the city and Levis was made by Admiral Holmes about the middle of July, though previous to this Wolfe and Saunders had passed up in an open boat to examine the nature of the approaches towards the rear of the city. Holmes having tested the chances of reaching the upper waters in safety by running one or two of his warships thither with several transports filled with troops, his whole division was soon finding safe moorage in the vicinity of Sillery.

8. *"To the masking of his pain."* The state of health of the General was well known to his colleagues, and no one can discount the important share which his three Brigadier-Generals must have taken in the military oversight of affairs.

9. *"From beyond Cap Rouge to Sillery."* One or two French vessels were in patrol beyond Cap Rouge, but they made no effort to check any of the sailing craft of Admiral Holmes.

10. *"While Bougainville would chide."* Louis Antoine Bougainville, a native of Paris, had made a name for himself in France, years before he was sent out to join Montcalm as a colonel of the French army in America. His record is a full one, not only as a soldier, but as a navigator and mathematician, his voyage round the world in 1770 making a stir in every part of the French world, much as Captain Cook's did in the English world. He has been

blamed for not making greater expedition in going to Montcalm's assistance, but the blame is altogether ill-founded, considering the suddenness of events. When one knows how he kept watch and ward up and down the river against the invaders, for so many weeks, without making a mistake, there is little reason to charge him with dilatoriness in action. Verger, who had charge of the post at the *Anse au Foulon*, was no subordinate of his, being of Vaudreuil's selection and oversight.

11. "*While Verger kept his outlook.*" It is said that Captain Verger had under him over one hundred men to guard the ascent from the Cove. These belonged for the most part to the militia of Lorette; and a memoir of the times tells us that several of these had obtained from their commanding officer a permit to return on a visit to their homes the night before Wolfe made his ascent. And in connection with Verger's neglect of his trust, there are many stories on record. It is said that he had been one of Bigot's creatures, and had sent away his men on purpose, since he knew his profligate master was anxious to see the colony come to grief in order to have his own iniquities buried in the ruins. Then, again, he is said to have been asleep in his tent when Wolfe's first advance reached his outpost, or that his sentinels were asleep when they should have been sounding the alarm. The story about the deceiving reply in French by one of Wolfe's officers who had learned to speak French in Flanders, given to the challenge from above, would go to show that there was some one awake and keeping guard in the vicinity of Verger's camp, however stupid he may have been not to suspect danger all the time. In the multiplicity of contradictory stories, it is safest for us to fall back upon the simple-worded, straightforward report of honest Captain John King, who speaks of events in this way: "The chain of sentries which they had posted along the summit of the heights galled us a little, and picked off several men, (in the boat where I was one man was killed); one seaman with four soldiers were slightly, and two mortally wounded, and some officers, before our light infantry got up to dislodge them." The true version seems to be that Verger's men first fired their muskets at the bateaux below, and then forsook their commanding officer, who had been seized by the Highlanders after their hand-over-hand

climb up the steep below the head of the Cove. At least honest John King tells us again: "We lost no time, but clambered up one of the steepest precipices that can be conceived, being almost perpendicular and of incredible length; and as soon as we gained the summit all was quiet, and not a shot was heard, owing to the excellent conduct of the infantry under Colonel Howe." The question therefore resolves itself into: Was John King one of the "hand-over-hand" men, and were these men under instructions from Colonel Howe, when they faced that "almost perpendicular" cliff to get at Verger's outpost? The unlucky Verger was taken prisoner, but never afterwards had a good word spoken of him by his compatriots. Indeed, Captain Verger is the Major André of the history of New France, whether he was guilty of treason to his country or only neglect of duty.

12. "*Beyond the Samos battery.*" The Samos roadway is an offshoot from the St. Louis Road near the modern village of Bergerville, and at the foot of it, near the shore of the river, there was a French battery, which is supposed to have challenged Wolfe's flotilla as it passed to the head of the *Anse au Foulon*, and to have been deceived by the phrase, "*Ces sont les vivres.*"

13. "*With no De Lévis nigh at hand.*" After the repulse at Montmorency, De Lévis had been sent to Montreal to watch the movements of Amherst in the west. (See biographical sketch).

14. "*Nor Bourlamaque the bold.*" Brigadier-General Bourlamaque came out to Canada at the instance of the French Governor as a colonel of engineers. He was present at the Battle of Carillon, where he led Montcalm's left wing to victory and was severely wounded. A like fate befell him at the Battle of Sainte-Foye, where, while leading his men to the defeat of the British under General Murray, he was again severely wounded, having had his horse killed as he fell from it in the rush of the onset. In after years he became Governor of Guadaloupe. (See biographical sketch).

15. "*Only Vaudreuil discordant.*" Pierre François Vaudreuil (pronounced *Vodroy*), was a native of Quebec, having been born there in the year 1698. He was therefore a man of sixty-one when troublous times came to him in the vicinity of his native

town in 1759. He had been trained for military service, having attained to the rank of major in the marine service in his earlier days. The contrast between his peevish criticism of Montcalm's conduct at Carillon, and his courage in pleading for a rallying under Bougainville, show the cross-lights in his character. There was certainly an unfortunate lack of sympathy between him and Montcalm—jealousy on the part of Vaudreuil, and possibly contempt on the part of the latter—which could not but be prejudicial to the French cause; the blame lying for the most part with Vaudreuil's martinetcy and presumption—advising over often, as he did, when advice was unnecessary, and interfering when interference could only provoke friction.

16. *"The bitterness for Montcalm."* There was not a little restlessness within the Beauport lines on account of the uncertainty in the delivery of supplies, now that the British were known to be intercepting them up the river. There was also a stream of desertions from among the peasant soldiers, who were unable to withstand periodical attacks of home-sickness, when they heard of the ravages being made by the British rangers in the country districts where their farms lay. The condition of affairs in the city itself was also becoming more and more deplorable, from sickness and rapine. On more than one occasion it was necessary to hang some of the neglectful sentinels and military marauders. Nor were Montcalm's own premonitions void of disquietude, though those around his camp at Beauport could detect in him no sign of over-solicitude. In a letter to his cousin, written a few weeks before his last battle, he utters the ominous prophecy: "If M. Wolfe understands his business, he has only to receive my first fire, give a volley in return, and then charge; when my Canadians —undisciplined, deaf to the sound of the drum, and thrown into confusion by his onset—would be incapable of resuming their ranks. Moreover, as they have no bayonets with which to oppose those of the enemy, nothing would remain for them but flight; and then—behold me beaten. Conceive my situation! A most painful one for a General-in-Chief, and which causes many distressing moments."

17. *"Five thousand strong."* There is a great diversity in the many computations that have been made concerning the numbers

of the contending forces in the immediate contest on the Plains of Abraham. The Britishers must have numbered over four thousand, while the French and Canadian musters on the field could not have been much less than twice that number.

18. *"Is that the pibroch of the Celtic braves?"* Sergeant James Thompson, who was present at the Battle of the Plains of Abraham, has left in his copious diary the following somewhat amusing anecdote: "We had but one piper, and because he was not provided with arms and the usual other means of defence, like the rest of the men, he was made to keep aloof for safety. When our line advanced to the charge, General Townshend, observing that the piper was missing, and knowing well the value of one on such occasions, sent in all directions for him, and was heard to say aloud: "Where's the Highland piper? Five pounds for a piper!" But never a bit did the piper come forward the sooner. However, the charge was pretty well effected without him, as all those that escaped could testify. For this business the piper was disgraced by the whole of the regiment, and the men would not speak to him, neither would they suffer his rations to be drawn with theirs, but had his served out by the Commissary separately. Thus was he obliged to shift for himself as best he could." Nor was it until next spring, in the Battle of Sainte-Foye, that the said piper was restored to favour, when he succeeded in rallying the courage of a section of Murray's forces sufficiently to allow of their being brought back to some sort of order during the retreat to the city. "For this opportune blast of his chanters," says Sergeant Thompson, "the piper gained back the forgiveness of the regiment, and was allowed to take his meals with his old messmates, as if nothing at all had happened."

19. *"The spot revered."* This is ever the objective point of the tourist's visit to Quebec. Everything is of intense interest in the neighbourhood of James Wolfe's Monument—the second one erected—which tells its own simple story. The well from which a cup of water was drawn to cool the lips of the dying General has been located near by Battlefield Cottage, now in the hands of a branch of the Dominicans, and situated only a short distance from the grassy slope on which the victorious hero breathed his last. The place provides an excellent centre for the Battlefields Historic Park.

20. *"To sift the cannon's boom."* As has been said, there was but one gun drawn up the bed of the Ruisseau St. Denis by the British on to the heights the morning of the battle, and the silencing of the French guns compared with the booming of that solitary gun might have been taken by the dying General as some indication of how the battle was going.

21. *"Ah, no, for stands a messenger."* The message was delivered by Lieutenant Brown, of the Louisbourg Grenadiers, who was standing near the prostrate General with those who had carried him to the rear.

22. *"From Louisbourg victorious wave."* The Grenadiers had been at the taking of Louisbourg with Amherst and Wolfe in 1758, where they had crowned their several charges with much glory, Wolfe then holding rank as Brigadier-General.

23. *"Send Burton."* This was Colonel Burton, who during the campaign had first had charge of the Levis batteries, and who on the morning of the battle had been placed in charge of a battalion of Royal Americans near the Ste. Foye Road to meet the advance of Bougainville, should he arrive from Cap Rouge before the engagement was over.

24. *"To guard St. Charles's bridge."* This was the bridge of boats which was anchored up the St. Charles, behind the dismantled vessels and boom, which were situated near where the present Dorchester Bridge spans the river. The bridge itself was placed a short distance below where the Bickell Bridge now crosses over from Hare Point to the modern village of Stadacona. It had direct connection with the horn-work now to be seen on the Ringfield property.

25. *"His deeds would joyous ring."* The British nation went wild with joy when the frigate arrived in London bearing the news of the victory and the remains of the dead General. A public funeral was appointed by royal decree, and a place set apart for a monument to Wolfe in Westminster Abbey.

26. *"Sainte-Foye gives tongue across the plain."* The troop that suffered most in this flank movement on the part of the French and Indian sharpshooters in the Ste. Foye woods was Colonel Burton's Royal Americans.

27. *"With Wolfe and Montcalm stricken down."* The death of Wolfe, in accordance with his own dying wish, was not communicated to the army until the battle was over, Townshend assuming supreme command only when the news went round that General Monckton, Wolfe's second in command, had been disabled almost immediately after the death of his commander-in-chief. Montcalm received his death-wound while he was striving to restore some kind of order in the retreating ranks of his panic-struck troops. He was on horseback at the time, and was borne with the crowd through St. Louis Gate down St. Louis Street, to the house of Dr. Arnoux, which stood near where the St. Louis Hotel now stands. It is said that it was in the house of Dr. Arnoux he breathed his last, early in the morning after the battle.

28. *"And when Ramézay sought his couch."* Montcalm's last message was delivered in the hearing of the Commandant of the Citadel, who was also colonel of the Royal Rousillons. Chevalier de Ramézay had been in command in the city all during the siege, assuming at times the functions of Governor Vaudreuil during his absence at Beauport.

29. *"Awhile becrowned with emblem of the law."* The jail of Quebec was finished in 1867 at an expense of one hundred and forty thousand dollars. From its site an excellent view is to be had of the battlefield. The jail grounds cover an area of thirty-two acres, extending to the headlong steep of the river's bank.

30. *"With the famæ which they bring."* Few cities of the size of Quebec have had so much written about them as has the ancient capital of Canada, and it is a pity that a complete collection of these writings has never been made in any of the city's libraries.

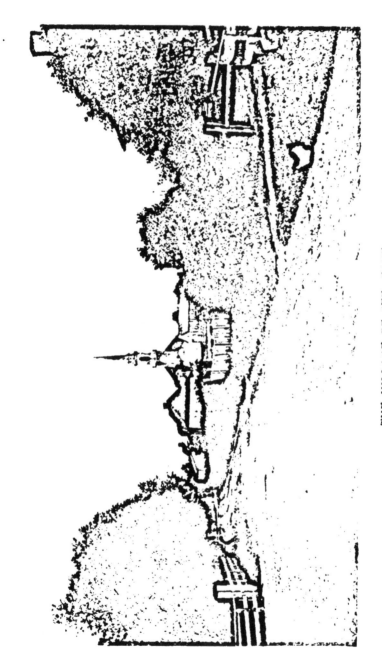

THE VILLAGE OF STE. FOYE

The Battle of Sainte-Foye

THE THIRD CONTEST

Introduction to Third Contest

THE site of the Battle of Sainte-Foye is of wider scope than that of the Battle of the Plains, the preliminary movements of the besiegers having been conducted for the most part on the land side, after De Lévis and Vaudreuil had sent the large body of their troops from Montreal by river, as far as Pointeaux-Trembles, from which the land march was made. Some of the transports conveying these troops found their way on the morning of the battle as far as Wolfe's Cove, though the great bulk of the army marched overland from Cap Rouge and the river parishes above, on their way to the city or General Murray's outworks.

From the Dufferin Terrace there diverge three main thoroughfares, which the reader should try to identify in the clearest manner possible. Two of these run all but parallel, after the one has passed through St. Louis Street and the other through Fabrique Street and St. John Street, out into the open country, as far as Cap Rouge, where they coalesce. The third highway traverses lower town from the base of the cliff on which the terrace has been erected, extending by way of St. Peter Street, St. Paul Street, and St. Joseph Street, and thereafter extending through the villages or parishes of Little River, Ancient Lorette and St.

7 93

Augustin, towards Pointe-aux-Trembles, Pont Rouge, and Portneuf. A drive by way of the first mentioned highways, out by the St. Louis Road and in by the Ste. Foye, will give the visitor a very good idea of the "lay of the land" over which De Lévis and Murray had to lead their forces before they met in battle shock on or near the plain where Wolfe contended with Montcalm.

After the departure of the British fleet in October, 1759, carrying with it Townshend and Saunders—the embalmed body of Wolfe having been sent immediately to England in the frigate which carried the despatches announcing the victory to the king and his ministers— the captured city was left in the keeping of General James Murray. Neither De Lévis nor Bougainville had been able to arrive in time to the support of Mont- calm on the fateful thirteenth of September; but it soon came to be noised abroad that as soon as spring brought the right kind of weather, the former would take Montcalm's place as commander-in-chief, and, with Bougainville and Bourlamaque as his next in command, would make resolute endeavour to retake the town, and re-assure Vaudreuil in his governorship.

To protect the approaches by any of the three main highways just referred to, General Murray established his outposts of defence at Ste. Foye church and Lorette, which should keep their eye upon any inroad from St. Augustin and Calvaire, as well as Cap Rouge. When De Lévis did appear on the scene, Murray was com- pelled, by the strength of numbers, to evacuate these outposts. The army opposing him numbered nearly nine thousand, at least De Lévis was known to have largely augmented the army he had brought together in Montreal, on his way down the river in a fleet of improvised war-craft and bateaux, as well as by land.

The arrival of De Lévis towards the approaches to Quebec was almost as sudden as Wolfe's had been, when he led his men up the steeps of the *Anse au Foulon*, though Murray had time to marshal his forces on the Buttes-à-Neveu, in timely anticipation of his enemy's battle array. The British left wing, which included Kennedy's and Bragg's divisions and Lascelles' Highlanders, was placed in charge of Colonel Fraser; while the right wing, including the divisions of Amherst, Anstruther, and Webb, with a battalion of Royal Americans, was under the command of Colonel Burton. Colonel Young had charge of the Reserves; Major Dalling, the Light Infantry; and Captain Macdonald, the Rangers.

De Lévis was not given time to arrange his army, wing to wing, and in battle array, against Murray's lines, as Wolfe had faced Montcalm's. The French vanguard had only just reached the heights above Wolfe's Cove, busying themselves ·in renewing the trenches which Wolfe's soldiers had formerly dug out— the main body of the French army being still on the march by the Ste. Foye Road—when Murray ordered an advance all along his line from the Buttes-à-Neveu. Before the British had come to close quarters with their opponents, however, the French vanguard had succeeded in spreading themselves across the plateau from their redoubts on the St. Louis Road to Dumont's Mill on the Ste. Foye Road, while the remaining French brigades hastened in close order along the parallel highways to support the thin line of the vanguard.

The first onset on the part of Murray caused De Lévis to withdraw his brigades within the shelter of the woods to the west of what is now the line of the Belvedere Road. This movement Murray mistook for a sudden retreat, such as had happened on the line of De Salaberry Street seven months before. Consequently, he pressed forward across a ground where the melting snow had made every kind of footing insecure—an impossible place for men or guns in advance or retreat. This was Murray's fatal mistake. The Light Infantry under Major Dalling were driven hither and thither over this ground, unable to re-form before the French came out from their shelter, to attack them as well as Murray's right and left wings. When once Dumont's Mill fell into the hands of the French, the fight from the one highway to the other became a mixed and general one, with the most serious carnage round the Mill.

The closing scenes of the battle were but an outnumbering of Murray's disordered lines. The General stubbornly sought to strengthen his right wing near the Mill, by drawing one or two companies for relief from his left, doing his best to re-occupy the Mill. But as soon as De Lévis saw this, he ordered a bayonet charge to be directed against Murray's weakened left, as well as the retention of the Mill irrespective of the carnage that it involved. The bayonet charge was so irresistible that Murray's left wing was driven from the St. Louis Road on to the Ste. Foye Road; and, when the British wings thus became mixed and somewhat huddled, a reserve brigade of the Royal Rousillons made a final strenuous attack on the huddled mass of Murray's troops, and drove them in the greatest disorder along the Ste. Foye Road towards the city.

The battle had lasted over an hour and a half, some say longer, the numbers on the one side having been three thousand, according to General Murray's verified statement, while those on the French side could not have been less than double that number.

The *Monument-aux-Braves* is the prominent landmark that commemorates the event of the Battle of Sainte-Foye, erected as it has been where the strife raged at its bitterest, and where the carnage caused the stream that ran by Dumont's Mill to run red with blood. And it is from this spot that the plan of the battle may be seen most conveniently in its inner aspects. The outlook from its immediate neighbourhood is certainly worthy of examination by those who desire to study the topography of such an important event in the history of the country. And, in behalf of the reader, the following paragraph may be appropriately quoted from the same writer who introduced us to the marvels of the outlook from the Dufferin Terrace while yet the snow was on the ground:

"Beyond the limits of the level ground, the hills rise up terrace-like, bright even in the late autumn with the verdure of gardens, and rendered still more attractive by the endless succession of villas, farmhouses, and villages which dot the rising ground at intervals until they are lost in the distance, far away in the rear behind Jeune Lorette, Charlesbourg, and Beauport, where the blue summits of the Laurentian range rise to the skies. On the left, at one end of the valley, the prospect is rendered still more grand by the mountain heights and thickly wooded fringes of the farm-land undulations, bright as these are in the autumn with their orange crimson and russet tints."

Altogether, it is a locality of surpassing natural beauty, one that cannot but enhance the delight of the student-visitor, as he or she spells out the lesson of a great historical turning-point, on the very spot where a bold and brave attempt was made to perpetuate a regime that had evidently outlived its days, though not its sense of chivalry and courage and persistency of purpose.

The Battle of Sainte-Foye

Alas! how strange the blending of the best and
    worst in man,
When the victor and the vanquished pause, their
    cruelties to scan,
While the glare of hate is in their eye, with the
    war-rage still aflame,
To turn the tide of dire retreat or amplify ac-
    claim!
Is there aught but pride Satanic in this devil's dance
    of war—
In this pitting of the passions, a realm to make or
    mar?

The city has been taken, as 'twas taken once
    before,[2]
With woe for those who lost it, with joy for con-
    queror;
This time with dead and dying and famine sore
    within,
With no asset from the blood-stained strife, save
    the echoes of the din;
But what of that if heroes live, to replace the heroes
    slain?
Or who will say the country's lost,[3] though the
    city has been ta'en?

'Tis months since Wolfe and Montcalm fell, brave
    rivals in the field,
The one in triumph borne to rest upon a nation's
    shield,
The other humbly coffined near, within the Ursu-
    line,[4]
Where the penitent still count their beads, and the
    pious prize their shrine;
And all the while brave Murray holds the reining
    in his hand,
And all the while brave Lévis plans, to widen his
    command.

And as these soldiers daily read what legacies are
    theirs,
The one prepares for onset, while the other counts
    his cares,
Withstanding disaffection, as he fortifies the town,
Allotting purpose in his plans to re-assure renown.
Ah, how the weary months[5] for him are laden with
    surmise,
As the balance dips on either side, when rumour
    hope defies!

There was watching, ceaseless watching, from the
    outposts far and near,
Sainte-Foye defiant of Cap Rouge, and Old Lorette
    Calvaire;[6]
And should surprise come creeping from the Pointe-
    aux-Trembles camp,
Down either side the river's bed, alarm was wont
    to ramp,
Presaging but one tale to tell—the tale of driving
    back—[7]
A tale of courage-quickening for a final close attack.

And need there was for quickening, as the winter
    months went by,
With Arctic shafts a-piercing keen, as from an
    enemy,
With the city half in ruins[8] and the rations run-
    ning low,
With pallid penury and death a-stalking to and fro.
Alas! how strange the blending of the best and
    worst in man,
When the victor and the vanquished pause, the
    effects of war to scan!

.   .   .   .   .   .

The April sun has spent its warmth upon the swirl-
    ing floes,
And the sentry near the Cul-de-Sac,[9] as his pacing
    comes and goes,
Is thinking, with his comrades, that relief may miss
    its chance,
Should the river's icy products keep up their maze-
    like dance,
Making checking in the channel, and a hindrance
    to the shore,
While hope within the city's walls grows a-weary
    more and more.

To the southward by the Chaudière's vale,[10] a mes-
    senger is sent,
To the westward down the harbour, the *Lawrence*
    makes descent,"[11]
Not in terror but from foresight, to hasten prom-
    ised aid,
From Amherst or from Colville's fleet,[12] against
    prospective raid,
Should the later silence of the foe be taken to portend
The mustering of outnumbering host, along the
    river's trend.

The wind is fanning lazily the ice-floes making chase,
As the sentry near the Cul-de-Sac keeps a-mending
    of his pace:
The darkness draws a springtide sheen, from the
    corpse-like cakes afloat,
As a creaking cadence all their own they make
    athwart the moat.
"Hark! What is that? Can aught alive be haz-
    arded out there?
"What, ho, the guard! Advance at once, and in
    the rescue share!"

And the call disturbs the guardsmen in the bar-
    racks near at hand:[13]
There is haste in every movement and a rushing
    towards the strand:
"A boat! a boat!" the sentinel cries: "ne'er pause
    for reason why.
"There's some one caught in the drifting ice: I
    hear his piteous cry:
"Yea, yonder! Pull no lingering stroke, within,
    without, beyond,
"Ploughing the clefts in the clinging floes! Ah,
    ha, what 'tis you've found?"

How momentous was their finding—'twas a sol-
    dier helpless, cold—
Took time to piece it out, as his faltering tale was told.
'Twas a sergeant, from the squadron on its way
    from Montreal,[14]
Who, while wrestling with the darkness, met mis-
    fortune in a squall; .
Alas! his comrades had been drowned, 'mid the
    raging of the night,
Ere he had crept on the drifting ice, his only hope
    in sight.[15]

Nor was his story ended, till confession he had
    made
How De Lévis with his army, full purposed for
    blockade,
Was on his way to reach Cap Rouge, where his
    boats at anchor lay,
To supplement his armament in the coming final fray:
"Even now his light-draft galiots may be seeking
    nearer ground,
"In the *Anse au Foulon*,[16] where of late the British
    landing found."

And soon the tidings swift were borne to General
    Murray's ear,
In his chamber in the Chateau, and carried far
    and near,
To every quarter of the town, from the barracks
    to the gates,
With instant orders flying fast from each soldier
    to his mates:
"Arm, arm, and muster in the square, for imme-
    diate march at dawn:
"The General's word must be obeyed, though the
    news be overdrawn!"

"If, decimate by sickness, 'tis ours to brave the test:
"We have comrades keeping watch and ward on
    the highways to the west:
"The General leads in person, and in him there's
    ample trust;
"Besides, 'tis better far for us to dare defeat than
    rust:
"In their frequent winter skirmishings we have
    beaten them so far,
"And now the chance is ours at last to determin-
    ate the war."

'Twas thus the soldiers had their say, and the citizens as well,
Though what the latter thought *intime* is hardly safe to tell:
They were loathe to change their masters, though well they knew with pain,
How Bigot and his entourage had been New France's bane,[17]
How, with his deviltries a-rage, daring decency a-face,
The credit of the old regime had been blighted with disgrace.

Yea, thus the soldiers had their say, and the citizens as well,
Though what the General had in mind no gossip could reveal.
His countenance showed no alarm at the sergeant's final word,
Nor was he turned from counsels wise by the volubly absurd.
His duty was to reach Cap Rouge, to impede the near advance
Of De Lévis as he strode ahead, his prowess to enhance.

Nor did he fail to tell the town, with siege now imminent,
'Twere best non-militants withdrew, to lessen the lament
Of being sacked by kin their own, while the die was being cast,
Whether the old or new regime the other should outlast—
To lessen the temptation of betraying England's cause,

From an instinct all untrained as yet to prize an
    ally's laws.

" 'Tis the General who has ordered!" cry the exiles
    on their way
Beyond the streets and gateways, seeking refuge
    as they may;
"The cruel-hearted Murray!" sobbed the matrons
    in distress,
With their children clinging round them, in the
    hither-thither press;
"Some have called *ces anglais* faithless, but now
    we know 'tis true,
"With our very own the victims of their *perfidié-
    perdue!*"[18]

"Our homes again are devastate; woe, woe, to us
    and ours!
"Has *la bonne Marie* forsaken us, while war its
    woe outpours,
"Upon our broken citizenship? Oh, save us, God
    on high,
"From the burden of this bitter strife, wherein
    'tis death we buy!"
Alas! how strange the blending of the best and
    worst in man,
When the victor and the vanquished pause, war's
    cruelties to scan!

   .   .   .   .

Near the edging of the highway, emerging from
    its shade,
Where the brooklet of the Belvedere[19] makes a
    varying cascade,
While the springtide snows are melting and the
    maples throb with sap,

And all nature seems a-dusting the winter from
    its lap,
Can we unravel the traditions of that brooklet
    running blood,
When the victor and the vanquished here, each
    other's rage withstood?

Some will marvel at the carnage in no ecstasy of
    pride,
Since triumph and discomfiture had here a change
    of side:
With September's duel set at nought by De Lévis
    and his *braves*,
'Twas a valour daring valour up to where discre-
    tion saves—
The vanquished claiming victory and the victor
    in retreat,
With no change in old Dame Fortune's plans to
    amplify the feat.

There is presage of reversal in the prelude to the
    storm
Decreed to burst, alas, again, when once the armies
    form
On the field, perchance, where destiny decrees a
    brotherhood,
From the rivalries of nations, by a baptism of blood.
For when the British outposts of Cap Rouge and
    Old Lorette
Have found first shelter at Sainte-Foye, the bugle
    sounds retreat.[20]

And soon recurring history is on the stand again,
Making music for the nations in the same old cal-
    lous strain:

Two armies, one three thousand strong, the other
    twice its might,
On the plain where Wolfe and Montcalm fought,
    with death for both in sight:
Brave Murray with his forces ranged, where Mont-
    calm made survey
Of his rival's troops drawn up for him, in their
    thin-lined red array.

De Lévis' plans were soon revealed, when his van
    ranged from the *Anse*,
Where his frigates were in moorage,[21] to supple-
    ment the advance
Of his main line by the highways that paralleled
    the crest
Of the plateau running to Cap Rouge, from the
    city east and west:
"I must surprise him wing by wing," said Murray
    in his haste,
"God giving nerve unto my men as they march
    across the waste!"

"Hie yonder, Major Dalling, take up the first at-
    tack,
"While their van is busy digging, and their right
    is finding track,
"To marshal west of Dumont's Mill,[22] where the
    Grenadiers defend,
"And keep your muster well in hand, while the
    northern wings contend."
Thus ordered General Murray, as he battle-signal
    gave,
Hoping to time the marching to check each onward
    wave.

"Make for their left," De Lévis cried, "and press
    them south and north,
"Between the plateau's highway-lines, while our
    centre sallies forth,
"In detachments from the thickets, with all bayo-
    nets in place,
"To rake each wing with shot and steel, and thus
    their van efface!"
And now both armies interlock, with passion loose
    of rein,
Led by the brave against the brave under heroic
    strain.

Rage unto rage the knolls resound, life for a life
    defies,
The wounded in their anguish have no tending
    to their cries:
Hither and thither, pursuit, retreat are hasting
    o'er the plain,
The Mill is ta'en, the melee's mixed, the Mill is
    ta'en again;
And all the while brave Murray holds the reining
    in his hand,
And all the while brave Lévis plans, to widen his
    command.

Into the woods and back again, the invaders muster
    make,
While Burton, Fraser, and the rest their courage
    overtake—
When Bourlamaque is stricken down,[23] and his
    men still hold their own,
To rally round the Grenadiers, their wavering to
    condone—
When Repentigny fierce attacks the lines[24] of
    steadfast Young,—

When brave La Corne outvies the zeal our poets
    oft have sung.[25]

From wing to wing outnumbered, the British feel
    the strain
Of tumult knocking at their pride, athwart the
    gory plain:
Nor was the General slow to note a wavering in
    their pride,
When Dalling's broken cohort failed to rally to
    his side,
Up to the time the Rousillons rushed down on
    Burton's wing,
And De Lévis sounded full advance, as a message
    from the king.

'Twas a victory, say you; nay, a rout—the brave
    against the brave,
The vanquished now in full pursuit of their vic-
    tors' broken wave:
The carnage left to be enhanced by the devil and
    his mates,[26]
With an only refuge near at hand, within the city's
    gates.
'Twas a victory, say you; nay, a rout—the brave
    against the brave:
The baptism of blood, alas! our brotherhood to
    save!

And where we linger stood the Mill when the storm
    was at its worst,
Where now for us the veerie makes its song within
    the hurst:

8

Where the brook makes secret murmurings within
    its summer bed,
As if no slaughter e'er had dyed its waters crim-
    son red,
Nor the Laurentides had ever looked upon the
    seeming hell
Of the brave in the gripe of bravery, under Sa-
    tanic spell.

And still the brooklet wakes our pride on the spot
    where nations bled,
Where the Monument stands sentinel near the
    brooklet's narrow bed;
Ay, here we con our heroes' names and read tra-
    dition's praise,
With no ceasing in the soul's refrain, as still we
    stand and gaze:
Alas! how strange the blending of the best and
    worst in man,
When the victor and the vanquished pause, war's
    cruelties to scan.

Notes on "The Battle of Sainte-Foye"

1. *The name Sainte-Foye.* Whatever connection there is in the names, it may be brought to mind that a stir was caused in Quebec, as early as 1625, over the possession of an Indian boy who had been a favourite of Father Nicholas. The urchin was for a time an inmate of the Recollet Monastery, the Jesuits bidding for his possession, and even Emery de Caën wishing to take him to France under his patronage. The Jesuits ultimately secured him as their prize through the intercession of their patron, the Duc de Ventadour. "They made the most of their acquisition," as Dr. Douglas says, "for the little fellow, after such instruction in the faith as could be given by a lay teacher, was baptized with much ceremony in the cathedral of Rouen, under the name of Louis de Sainte-Foye. The Duc de Longueville and Madame de Villars stood as god-parents, and the crowd filled the sacred pile to see the son of a Huron king and the heir-apparent to a vast domain, as the sailors reported him to be, received into the arms of Holy Church. It was a fitting counterblast to the Protestant baptism of Pocahontas and her marriage to John Rolfe." One of the surnames of Louis XIII was Sainte-Foye, or Good-Faith. The church, which Murray took possession of, was known as the Church of Notre Dame de Ste. Foye.

2. *"It was taken once before."* Quebec was taken by Sir David Kirke in 1629, Champlain's capitulation involving no loss of human life. Sir William Phips thought to wrest it from Frontenac in 1690, but was repulsed; while Sir Hovenden Walker, with a like object of laying siege to the place in 1711, was prevented from doing so by a disastrous storm in the gulf, which all but destroyed his fleet. The siege of Wolfe's day may therefore be looked upon as the third siege of Quebec.

3. *"Or who will say the country's lost?"* Lord Amherst, at the time of the siege by Wolfe, was in the west, De Lévis was at Montreal, while Bourlamaque was on the Richelieu, so that there was much to be done to wrest the government from Vaudreuil, even after the victory of 1759.

111

4. *"Within the Ursuline."* The Convent of the Ursulines has its main entrances on Parloir and Stadacona Streets, which, together, make a circuit from St. Louis Street into Garden Street. The first building of the Convent was erected in 1641, two years after the arrival of Madame de la Peltrie and her associate *religieuses*, who had lodgings at first in a house on Notre Dame Street. The grounds on which the present spacious buildings stand, was a gift from the Company of the Hundred Associates, and includes an area of seven acres, the extent of the buildings within not being seen from the outer thoroughfares of Garden, Anne, and Ursule Streets, whose lines of houses enclose the grounds on three sides as with an outer wall. The original building was destroyed by fire eleven years after its erection, and the more spacious edifice raised on its site was also destroyed in the same way in 1686. The oldest sections of the present buildings date back to that time, having escaped the devastations of the siege of 1759, though the main entrance and the chapel on Stadacona Street have been rebuilt since 1880. The remains of Montcalm, removed as they may have been from his improvised grave in the grounds, if they ever had such a first sepulchre, were deposited within the area of the chapel, while a mural tablet was put in place by Lord Aylmer to the memory of the French general on the hundredth anniversary of his death. The place is one of the deepest interest to the visitor. (See the biography of General Montcalm.)

5. *"The weary months."* After Quebec was taken, it was seriously discussed, in a council of war, whether it was expedient to retain it or not, so dilapidated were its means of defence. When it was decided that General Murray should be left in command, steps had at once to be taken to bring some kind of order out of chaos. The winter, in its severity, was a first difficulty to contend with. As there was a scarcity of fuel, measures had to be adopted to employ the soldiers in hauling it in from the neighbouring woods. In these operations, the extreme cold often disabled a whole company of men by frost-bite; and on occasions when detachments were sent out on military duty against the enemy's outposts, as many as a hundred were at times brought back to be placed in the hospital. Nor was there lack of fever, dysentery, and scurvy in the town during these dreary winter months. The number of men fit for duty was reduced from seven

thousand and odd to three thousand, when arrangements had to be made to meet the enemy in open field. Garneau, the French historian, claims that there were 7,714 British present at the battle, which is simply an absurd reckoning, even had Murray said nothing about his depleted garrison in his despatches. In March, the hospitals were overcrowded with patients from the several regiments, the sturdy Highlanders being as severely stricken as the others, until Murray had to disallow all skirmishing against the outposts of the enemy. In addition to all this, there was serious unrest as well as sickness among the inhabitants of the town, not to speak of their tampering with the loyalty and morality of the soldiery, and the additional suffering arising from the rigorous measures which had to be adopted to check irregularity of conduct when it was detected.

6. "*Sainte-Foye defiant of Cap Rouge.*" The Church of Ste. Foye is situated about five miles out from the town, while Cap Rouge is about four miles further on. Ancienne Lorette is on the outer of the three main highways mentioned elsewhere, while St. Augustin is six or seven miles further on, with Calvaire near Lake Calvaire. Before De Lévis appeared upon the scene, Murray had established detachments at Ste. Foye and Lorette, and one night about the middle of March, there was a serious contest at Calvaire, in which over a hundred French militiamen were taken prisoners and several killed. (See Maps at end of volume.)

7. "*The tale of driving back.*" Several events, similar to the foregoing, had been occurring at intervals during the winter months. As early as November, Captain Walsh had made reprisal on Pointe-aux-Trembles, and later on a detachment of French volunteers, numbering five hundred or so, were driven from their entrenchments on the Levis side, with considerable loss in killed and wounded, the post being subsequently strengthened by a company of two hundred of Murray's men. In all of these and other minor engagements the English were the victors.

8. "*The city half in ruins.*" The town was in a pitiable plight after that almost continuous attack for months by the batteries of Levis and the guns of the fleet. When the memorable siege of 1759 began, there were only about nine thousand of a non-militant population in the place; and, when it was over, these

people, sadly reduced in numbers, were in a state of abject poverty until some settled way of earning a livelihood had been provided for them in the rebuilding of the town and the revival of trade. There were few of the houses along the lines of the streets, and none of the public edifices or churches that did not bear scars from the shot and shell of the invader. The thoroughfares were lumbered and encumbered with all kinds of debris, and all but impassable save to foot wayfarers. Hundreds of the residences were barely habitable, the rich and poor huddling anywhere for shelter as after a great fire or an earthquake. The places of worship were either overthrown or gutted. Trade was completely at a standstill. In a word, poor old Quebec was a city that had to be rebuilt from its very foundations. (See General Introduction.)

9. *"The sentry near the Cul-de-Sac."* The Cul-de-Sac was an inlet that is now occupied by the limits of the Champlain Market, bounded on the west by the King's Arsenal, where there was accommodation for some of the troops in garrison. It was used up to somewhat recent times as a mooring-place for small river craft, with wharfage along the line of Champlain Street.

10. *"To the southward of the Chaudière's vale."* The valley of the Chaudière was long the easiest route from Quebec to the New England colonies, a fact which Benedict Arnold took advantage of, fifteen years later, when he brought his troops to Quebec in 1775. The first messenger sent out by General Murray to reach the British winter quarters, by way of the Chaudière Valley, was a Lieutenant Butler, who, however, returned in ten days' time, to report that his snowshoe tramp towards New England had been interrupted by traces of Indians on the trail. The second messenger sent out was Lieutenant Montresor, who was accompanied by a band of rangers. He, passing up the Chaudière Valley, arrived in Boston in thirty days. The despatches he carried were placed in the hands of General Amherst, who was at New York at the time, and these finally reached Lord Colville, then the admiral of the British fleet stationed at Halifax and other ports along the North American coast line, and from whom Murray was looking for relief as soon as the winter ice would suffer ships to sail up the St. Lawrence as far as Quebec.

11. *"The Lawrence makes descent."* It was towards the latter end of April that the schooner *Lawrence*, the only seaworthy boat in Quebec harbour at the time, was sent down the river, to hasten Lord Colville and his fleet to the relief of the garrison, hemmed in, as the city was, from the moment De Lévis had appeared on the scene.

12. *"From Amherst or from Colville's fleet."* (See Notes 10 and 11.)

13. *"In the barracks near at hand."* Adjacent to the Cul-de-Sac stood the lower town barracks, which Murray had no doubt put in a state of repair for the accommodation of his own troops after he was placed in command of the garrisoned city at the instance of Monckton and Townshend.

14. *"On its way from Montreal."* These vessels included the frigates *La Pomone*, the *Atlanta*, and several sloops which had kept at a distance up the river, when once Admiral Holmes had succeeded in passing the city's batteries opposite Levis. According to the rescued sailor there was quite a fleet of galiots, floating batteries and bateaux, that had been sent from Montreal laden with ammunition, artillery, provisions, entrenching tools and stores of all kinds.

15. *"His only hope in sight."* This story has been variously told, and has even been altogether discredited. The following circumstantial account of the incident is given in the first volume of Smith's History of Canada. Smith's narrative rather impugns the poetic license of the stanza thus annotated, though it corroborates the main fact, and is worth quoting in full: "On the 27th of April, about two o'clock in the morning, the watch on board the war sloop the *Race Horse*, hearing a distressful noise on the river, acquainted Captain Cartney therewith, who instantly ordered out his boat, which shortly after returned with a man who had been found almost famished on a float of ice. Although all imaginable care was taken of him, he was above two hours before he could give an account of himself. When the terrors of his mind had subsided and he could speak, he gave his deliverer the intelligence, namely, that he was a sergeant of the French artillery, who, with six other men, were put into a floating battery of

an eighteen pounder; that his bateau was overset in a great
storm; that he swam and scrambled alternately through num-
berless floats of ice, until he met with a large one on which, though,
with great difficulty, he fixed himself; that he lay on it several
hours, passed the town with the ebb of tide, which carried him to
the church of St. Lawrence on the Island of Orleans; and was driving up again with the tide of flood at the time the boat happily
came to his relief; that the French squadron was on its way to the
Foulon at Sillery, where the troops on board were to disembark
to join the army of Lévis and Bourlamaque, amounting to twelve
thousand men; that the French fleet, particularly the small craft,
was broken up by the storm, and many vessels lost; that the general believed that they would be reinforced by a powerful fleet
and army from France; and that they were in the daily expectation of a frigate that had wintered at Gaspé laden with ammunition and stores."

16. *"In the Anse au Foulon."* The Anse au Foulon, or the Mill
Cove, was reached in early times by a roadway which passed across
the localized "Plains" so-called, and the Marchmont property,
the road being an offshoot from the St. Louis Road near the outlet
of the modern Maple Avenue. Had the guard there been strong
enough and fully on the alert, neither Wolfe, nor afterwards De
Lévis, could have found the easy access that they did to the levels
above at that point.

17. *"Bigot and his entourage."* Intendant Bigot's character
has been amplified in William Kirby's celebrated novel of Chien d'Or
—a character which elsewhere has been somewhat pithily summed
up in these words: "The man was a scoundrel and libertine in
private life, and a robber of the State and the people." He arrived in Canada in 1727, and his Intendancy extended up to the
time of the surrender of the whole country in 1760. After that
event he returned to France, where he and his associates were
thrown into the Bastille, from which he was only delivered to
be relieved of all his possessions and driven into exile. Bigot
was present at the siege of 1759, and on the arrival of Bougainville from Cap Rouge, took counsel with Vaudreuil and others to
renew the contest without delay. His *entourage* consisted of the
worst set of boodling tyrants Canada has ever known in ancient
or modern days.

18. *"From their perfidié-perdue."* The first to receive direct notice to leave the city were the Jesuit fathers, who were reported as having interfered in military matters. Their college buildings —so long known afterwards as the Jesuits' Barracks—were occupied, as soon as they were gone, as a magazine for provisions and military stores. Their expulsion was looked upon as worse than a *"perfidié-perdue"*: it was denounced as a sacrilege. Previous to this it had been given out that all who desired to leave the town might withdraw into the country parts with their families and household effects. When it was known that a second siege was imminent, the order was issued that all French residents should withdraw. As Dr. Miles says in one of his lucid footnotes: "Three days were allowed for the necessary preparations and removal. The people were directed to leave any of their effects they chose at the quarters of the Recollets, where two substantial citizens, appointed by the inhabitants, might remain to take care of them under the protection of a guard of soldiers. The urgent necessity of the measure was stated, and orders given that they should not come back until further notice. The inmates of two nunneries were allowed to remain, as they had been very useful in the care of the sick. The execution was made on the 24th and 25th of April, and was attended with much discomposure and distress. The male inhabitants were sullen, and prudently refrained from expressing their feelings; but the women were not so discreet. When their entreaties to be allowed to stay, coupled with promises to remain quiet, as well as to give the earliest information of De Lévis' proceedings, were disregarded, they exclaimed against what they affirmed was a manifest violation of the capitulation, adding: 'We have always heard the English called a faithless people; now we are convinced they are so.' Before the siege the population of the town was about 6,700. That portion of it which spent the winter within the walls must have been much less numerous. As showing Murray's precautions, though of a very stern character, were necessary in view of his own safety, the inhabitants of the country generally joined the forces of De Lévis in his subsequent siege of the place."

19. *"The brooklet of the Belvedere."* Like the Ruisseau St. Denis, the Belle Borne Brook, and sundry other streamlets on or near the Plains of Abraham, the Belvedere Brook makes quite a brattle

in early spring; though one wonders what benefit Miller Dumont had from its presence save that of drainage for his dwelling, his tannery and outhouses. M. Dumont's mill was probably driven by wind as other round towers in the neighbourhood of Quebec were, for the grinding of wheat and other cereals.

20. *"The bugle sounds retreat."* The account of this preliminary retreat of Murray's is best studied by itself, to avoid confusion in the reader's mind. It was a case of outnumbering, as was the after main engagement. De Lévis had arrived at Pointe-aux-Trembles, and had made up his mind to take possession of all of the three main highways leading to Quebec. To secure them he had to drive the English from their outposts at Cap Rouge, Lorette, and the Ste. Foye church. The latter outpost had been looked upon by the English as a place of retreat from Cap Rouge and Lorette, if necessity arose; but on the Sunday preceding the day of the battle proper, Murray led out thence from the town several large detachments, which he located in line to the south of the church towards the St. Louis highway, as if with the intention of trying conclusions with De Lévis at that point, after having called in the men at his outposts at Cap Rouge and Lorette. When once the French in overwhelming numbers concentrated towards the church, and were even yet thronging the woods and marshes leading to the sloping grounds of the plateau, Murray suddenly ordered the withdrawal of his whole armament back to the town. He had seen at a glance that the numbers of the enemy were too great for him to contend with successfully on such ground; and so leaving some of his fighting appliances, spiking his guns and setting fire to the church, he thought it best to re-encounter the melting snow-drifts and the slush on the way back, in order to rally a larger army nearer the city.

21. *"Where his frigates were in moorage."* As the shipwrecked gunner had declared, a section of the French ships and boats found their way to what now began to be called Wolfe's Cove, from which were disembarked De Levis' vanguard. This Murray attacked, before the main body of the French had arrived on the Plains. Some of these vessels were captured or destroyed by the English fleet, which arrived even while De Lévis was strengthening his entrenchments as if for a renewal of the struggle for

possession of the town, after the defeat of Murray. Knox, in his journal, tells us how *La Pomone* was handled in the same way up near Pointe-aux-Trembles. Only one small sloop is said to have escaped to Lake St. Peter.

22. *"To marshal west of Dumont's Mill."* The main attack in the Battle of Sainte-Foye took place on and off the line of what is now called the Belvedere Road, just as the shock of the Battle of the Plains between Wolfe and Montcalm took place off and on the line of what is now called De Salaberry Street.

23. *"When Bourlamaque was stricken down."* This brave soldier, to whom biographic reference is made elsewhere, was severely wounded in the battle by a cannon-shot as he was rushing with his men pell-mell towards Dumont's Mill. His men, however, did not halt in their course until they came to the rescue of their comrades under Captain Aiguebelles, as they were being decimated by the English artillery.

24. *"When Repentigny fierce attacks the line."* The brigade under this courageous leader brought their whole strength against the British centre, and has the credit of being the only brigade that maintained its ground during the whole time the obstinate struggle lasted.

25. *"The zeal our poets oft have sung."* La Corne de St. Luc and his troop showed wondrous staying powers during the contest, finally coming to the support of the Canadians of the Queen's Brigade in their attack on the main line of the British. Parkman observes in one of his footnotes, that the war in Canada produced a considerable quantity of indifferent verse on both sides, and subsequently quotes some of it.

26. *"By the devil and his mates."* The after carnage of the battle is referred to by Garneau in these words: "The savages, who were nearly all in the wood behind during the fight, spread out over the vacated battlefield while the French were pursuing the enemy, and they felled many of the wounded British, whose scalps were afterwards found upon the adjoining bushes. As soon as De Lévis was apprised of such cruelties, he took vigorous measures to put a stop to them. Within a comparatively narrow space

nearly two thousand and five hundred men lay dead on the field when all was over. The patches of snow and icy puddles were reddened with the bloodshed the frozen ground refused to absorb; while the wounded who had escaped the butchery of the savages were immersed in pools of gore and battle-filth all but knee-deep."

HÉBERT'S STATUE OF WOLFE

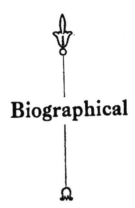

Biographical

Biography of General Wolfe

GENERAL JAMES WOLFE was a young man of only thirty-two years of age at the time of his heroic death on the historic Plains of Abraham, in 1759; and yet within that short span he had filled out in his person the career of a soldier which is rich enough in incident to fill a goodly-sized volume of close biographic detail. No school-day poem is any better known, perhaps, than *The Burial of Sir John Moore;* and the signature at the end of that poem takes us back to the story of James Wolfe's Irish ancestry in a very direct way, since the Rev. Charles Wolfe, once curate in a County Tyrone parish, who wrote these memorial lines on the hero of Corunna, was no other than the great-grand-uncle of the hero of Quebec.

As early as 1346, it is said that there were two families of the name of Wolfe in the south of Ireland, namely, the Wolfes of Kildare and the Wolfes of Limerick; and, in 1641, when Oliver Cromwell was making anything but popularity for himself among the Irish, it is on record that two brothers, George and Francis Wolfe, took a prominent part in the resistance to the cross-grained Protector during the siege of Limerick, in 1650. After the fall of Limerick, death by hanging was the fate that hung over those who had openly taken part in the siege as leaders. Among those con-

123

demned were the two brothers, George and Francis
Wolfe, the former being a soldier, the latter a friar in
training for the priesthood. Francis, the priest, was
hanged, but George escaped to the north of England,
and it was from him there sprang General James Wolfe,
the son of General Edward Wolfe, second in descent
from the escaped Limerick soldier.

Not content to trace the heroic General back to a
good and safe Irish origin, some of his biographers
claim that the Kildare Wolfes and the Limerick Wolfes
had a common Welsh origin. Be this as it may, at
the time of the Quebec Tercentennial Celebration,
one of the invited guests was a Lieutenant Wolfe, the
surviving nearest male relative of the distinguished
James Wolfe. This representative of the Wolfe family was of the Kildare side of the family, from which
there have sprung many prominent men tracing themselves back to the Irish branch of the family that still
has its country-seat at Forenaught, in the county of
Kildare, and another known as Cahivcondish, in the
county of Limerick.

Nevertheless, though James Wolfe can be proven
to have come from a good Irish stock, it would be idle
to attempt to locate any racial traces, either of his
far-away Irish origin or farther away Welsh origin,
in his character as an English soldier or citizen. He
was an Englishman in his life and bearing, born of an
English father and an English mother in 1727, in the
village of Westerham, in the county of Kent, and
within easy distance of London, where, during the
latter part of his eleven years' residence, he attended
the village school and enjoyed the comradeship of a
certain George Warde, from whom he seems to have

been grounded in his belief that there was no life for him but the soldier's life of his father, and that which the same George Warde had decided to take up with for himself. When the family removed from Westerham to Greenwich, and when young James Wolfe had had a year or two of a school training under the tuition of the Rev. Mr. Swindon, and further companionship with another schoolmate of the name of John Jervis, who afterwards became Lord St. Vincent of the British Admiralty, he was only too ready to join his father when, as adjutant-general, the latter was called to embark, with an army of ten thousand men, to take part in the Spanish war. The lad was only thirteen years of age at the time, and it is all but certain that he would have gone on that expedition, even at that early age and despite his mother's remonstrances, had there not been delay in the setting out of his father's troops. As it was, he returned home to Greenwich to spend another eighteen months or so with his mother and schoolmaster. There was nothing in his schoolboy days to indicate that the lad had in him what might help him to his after fame. He had made up his mind to be a soldier, and had his wish fulfilled even before he had reached his fifteenth year. It was while he was spending his Christmas holidays out at Squerryes Court, Westerham, with his former schoolmate, George Warde, that he received his first commission as ensign in his father's division, which was all but ready to set out for the continent.

From step to step, always upward and with exceptional distinction, the young officer advanced in his military career, which may thus be told in brief, up to the time he became second in command at Louisbourg and commander-in-chief at Quebec.

9

James Wolfe had his first lesson in active warfare in the war between France and Britain, as an ensign in Colonel Duroure's division, the 12th Regiment of Foot. This occurred in 1743, while the army was on its way from Ghent, to meet the French army on the battlefield of Dettingen, in Bavaria. And one can readily see how the main feature of the lesson clung to him, till he faced death in his last engagement on the Plains of Abraham, by reading one of his letters informing his father of the issue of the engagement: "The Major and I (for we had neither Colonel nor Lt.-Colonel), before they came near, were employed in begging and ordering the men not to fire at too great a distance, but to keep it until the enemy should come near us, but to little purpose. The whole fired when they thought they could reach them, which had like to have ruined us." The young ensign, however, was, immediately after the engagement, promoted to his lieutenancy.

Three years later, after having passed from his adjutancy, won by his personal bravery in the field, to the position of captain in the 4th Regiment, he is found in the capacity of brigade-major in Scotland, taking part in the battles of Falkirk and Culloden. In a book of Glasgow memoribilia an engraving is given of the house he occupied, and there lingers a legend that he once was stationed for a short time at the old Inversnaid Fort, on the road in the Rob Roy country, between the heads of Loch Lomond and Loch Katrine. There is also a legend about his refusing to obey the orders of the cruel-minded Duke of Cumberland on the field of Culloden, though there is only slender assurance that Wolfe took part in that engagement. The story, however, is that, while the Duke was passing across the battlefield after the Highlanders had been driven from it, what was left of them, his eyes came in line with those of a wounded Celt, who lay in his death struggle on the pathway. There was hatred and defiance in the dying soldier's face, and the enraged commander-in-chief ordered Wolfe, who was attending him as a newly-appointed major, to put the insolent fellow to death. But Wolfe is said to have instantly replied: "My commission is at your Royal Highness's disposal, but I can never consent to fulfilling the office of an executioner."

From Scotland he was called again to the continent, having been wounded in the battle of Laffelt, when again his personal bravery brought him after-promotion. At the age of twenty-two he attained to the command of the 20th Regiment, a something almost unheard of in the British army—such a young man in charge of a full regiment—yet it tells us how his ambitions, as betrayed in his letters to his parents and intimate friends, had for an objective only the highest preferment leading to the highest renown, in the profession he had been called to as if by instinct.

For a second time he was with his regiment in Scotland up to the year 1753, where again he made a name for himself as a shrewd and industrious military administrator. He is said to have been the first to counsel the banding of the restless Highlanders into regiments under distinctive Scottish titles, a policy which had very much to do with the directing of the pride of a proud people towards a new loyalty, and the bringing of fame to the British Empire through the bravery of its Highland regiments, notably, for example, of the Fraser Highlanders on the Plains of Abraham.

In 1757, he accompanied the expedition against Rochefort as quartermaster-general, and although the failure of that enterprise was due to lack of management, it was generally believed that, had Wolfe's counsels prevailed, the result would have been different, a favourable criticism which tended to enhance his reputation as a brave and capable officer. Indeed, so brilliant had his record as a soldier become by this time, that even in the face of a disaster to the British arms, he was given the full rank of colonel, and a few months later was found gazetted a brigadier-general, second in command to General Amherst, who had charge of the operations against the French in Cape Breton.

The successful issue of the siege of Louisbourg was the almost direct result of Wolfe's daring skill, so much so that he became popularly known as "the Hero of Louisbourg." The year after the fall of Louisbourg, plans were matured for a direct invasion of French Canada by way of the St. Lawrence. Things had been going from bad to worse in the hands of Abercrombie as leader of the British forces in America, and the British authorities, recognizing the superior qualities of Wolfe, placed him at the head of the expedition against Quebec, the capital of New France, bestowing upon him the high rank of major-general, and placing under his command over eight thousand troops.

His further record is the story of this book. With Admiral Saunders in command of the fleet, that expedition set sail from England on the 17th of February, 1759. Wolfe landed on the Island of Orleans with his army in full view of the city of Quebec, on the 26th of June. As we have seen, he lost no time, sick as he was from the long sea voyage, as he had always been when called upon to spend any time on board ship, to prepare his plans for attack, which, after two months of active operations, were at last crowned with success, though the carrying of them out cost him his life.

On the 13th of September, as we know, he succeeded in reaching the heights behind the city, whereon he spread out his well-ordered battle array against the French forces under General Montcalm. The result of that contest made it the most memorable event in the history of Canada; for after the short struggle, in which both leaders lost their lives, the British flag was raised on the stronghold of Quebec, and has continued to float there ever since, irrespective of the defeat of General Murray by General de Lévis in 1760, or the attempt of Montgomery and Arnold in 1775.

The life of James Wolfe presents a unique picture in itself, as we endeavour to find out from its inner tints what manner of a man he was. At the early age of thirty-two he had risen to the very highest prominence in his profession, and that as an immediate result of his own personal industry and ability. Through his father he had an influence, it is true, with those high up in the military counsels of the kingdom; but it is universally admitted that these would have been of but little avail in winning for him a name which pointed him out to the "Great Commoner," William Pitt, as the one man in sight for the successful guidance of the American War between the British and the

French into a final victory for the former. To what other eminence Wolfe might have risen had life been spared to him, is food for conjecture. As it is, he occupies a conspicuous place, one of the most conspicuous places, in the history of his country. And all his renown must not be traced to the outcome of one single event. As soon as the story of his greatest achievement had been borne across the Atlantic, he was acclaimed, as if by one common impulse, a deserving national hero. Parliament, at its first session after his glorious death, ordered a monument to be erected to his memory in Westminster Abbey. His embalmed body found a last resting-place in the family vault under Greenwich Parish Church. His mother was still alive when her son died, and the threads of romance attached to the widow's grief, and the interrupted prospect of his being married, had he returned to England alive, make up a story which even now has not lost its interest to the ordinary reader of romantic occurrences.

This romance and the minor details in the career of James Wolfe are those from which the true character of the man may be best detected, and these are found from the letters which have been saved of his from oblivion. He was one who had picked up his education between times, after he was done with the teachings of his mother and schoolmaster. His letters prove this, even his famous letter which embodies his own ideas of what constitutes "the whole duty of man" from the soldier's standpoint. In the most of them, soldierlike, he contents himself with a simple narrative of what has been going on around him either on the battlefield, or within the narrow circle of his acquaintances.   How considerately he deals with opposition on the part of his parents or others! He seemed always to have before him his duty towards others as a something that must not be allowed to interfere with his duty towards himself, which latter he was ever striving to uphold as his duty towards his country and his country's God. For instance, even when he was not more than thirteen, and had made up his mind to the taking up with the soldier's life, against the serious opposition of his mother, who would have him stay with her and his younger brother Edward at home for a year or two longer, he wrote home from the deck of the vessel that was to carry him on his first campaign, to the following effect, avoiding everything in the shape of offence to a wounded mother's authority:

"I will certainly write to you, dearest Mamma, and, when we are gone, by every ship we meet, because I know it is my duty. Besides, if it was not, I would do it out of love, with pleasure."

And again, when his brother Edward died, unable to bear up against the hardships of active service, which he had ventured upon, in emulation of his father's and elder brother's achievements in open field, the sorrowing brother wrote the news to the mother at Greenwich:

"Poor Ned wanted nothing but the satisfaction of seeing his dearest friends, as he was leaving this world with the greatest tranquillity. He often called upon us, and now it gives me many uneasy hours when I reflect on the possibility there was of my being with him before he died. God knows it was my being too exact, and not fully apprehending the danger the poor fellow was in; but even that would not have hindered me, had I received the physician's first letter. I know you won't be able to read this paragraph without shedding tears, as I do while writing it; but there is a satisfaction in giving way to grief now and then.

"There is, indeed, no part of poor dear Ned's life that makes him dearer to me than that where you have often mentioned—*he pined after me.* It often makes me angry that any hour of my life should pass without my thinking of him."

Thackeray, the distinguished novelist, in his *Virginians*, has striven, in a secondary kind of a way, to give us a vivid glimpse or two of the romance in James Wolfe's life; but it is again from his own letters we find the true story of his attachment to Miss Katherine Lowther, who after his death became the wife of the Duke of Bolton. This is how he writes of his romantic esteem for that lady to his friend Captain Rickson, in an exchange of confidences that it is now no betrayal to give in full. There is perhaps in it a little too much of the worldlimindedness that makes a menace to the higher ideal of love, but perhaps that arose from the character of the comrade of whom he was making a confessor:

"You will hear, in justice and return for your confidence, that I am not less smitten than yourself. The winter we were in London together, I sometimes saw Miss Lowther, the maid of honour, who is G. Mordaunt's niece. She pleased me then; but the campaign being in view, there was little time left me to think of love. The last time I was in town, which was only for three weeks, I was several times with her, sometimes in public, sometimes at her uncle's, and

two or three times at her own house. She made a
surprising progress in that time towards winning all
my affections. Some people reckon her handsome;
but I, that am her lover, do not think her a beauty.
She has much sweetness of temper, sense enough, and
is very civil and engaging in her behaviour. She
refused a clergyman with thirteen thousand a year,
and is at present having addresses paid to her by a very
rich knight; but in addition to what is your antagonist's misfortune, he has that of being mad, so that I
hold him cheap. In point of fortune she has no more
than I have a right to expect, viz., twelve thousand
pounds. The maid is tall and thin, about my own
age, and that's the only objection. I endeavoured,
with all the art I was master of, to find out how any
serious proposal would be received by Mordaunt and
her mother. It did not appear that they would be
very averse to such a scheme; but as I am but twenty-
two and three months, it is rather early for that sort
of a project; and, if I do not propose, somebody else
probably will. The General and Mrs. Wolfe are rather
against it, for other more interested views, as they
imagine. They have their eye on one for me of thirty
thousand pounds. If a company in the Guards is
bought for me, or I should be happy enough to purchase my lieutenant-colonel's commission within this
twelvemonth, I shall certainly ask the question; but
if I am kept long here the fire will be extinguished.
I have done with this subject and do you be silent
about it."

And the sequel of that story of a true love that didn't
run smooth, on account of the opposition to it from
both his father and mother, followed him up to the

night before his death. The wealthy maiden whom his mother had selected as a wife for her son, became engaged during Wolfe's residence in Scotland to his early playmate, John Warde; and it was while the London season was at its height, even while Wolfe on furlough was in the metropolis, that the master of Squerryes Court took his bride home to Westerham. This, of course, brought a pause to the efforts of Wolfe's parents to have their son marry for money. It also brought about a re-kindling of the soldier's love for Miss Lowther, who had been his own choice—a choice advanced to acceptance before he left for America, but which, alas, was not to be fulfilled.

Sir Gilbert Parker has ventured to limn, in his forcible English, the personal appearance of General Wolfe; and since the profile of the hero is no unidentifiable one from the many engravings and statues of him extant, the reader may be allowed to judge for himself of the truth of the novelist's analysis:

"Only the most invincible spirit could have borne so frail a body through these weeks of hope deferred," he says, referring to the delay in the siege. "A vague melancholy marked the line of his tall, ungainly figure; but resolution, courage, endurance, deep design, clear vision, dogged will, and heroism shone forth from those searching eyes, making of no account the incongruities of the sallow features. Straight red hair, a nose thrust out like a wedge, and a chin falling back from an affectionate sort of mouth, made, by an antic of nature, the almost grotesque setting of those twin furnaces of daring resolve, which, in the end, fulfilled the yearning hopes of England."

The familiar story of his floating down the river

towards Quebec, ou the most momentous occasion of his short life, while reading Gray's *Elegy*, need not be repeated here; nor can one help wondering why it has been repeated so often in the hearing of an age that is more or less inclined to laugh at the readers or writers of verse, unless the figures employed have been drawn from the ribaldries of the barracks-room or the gin-palace. Yet it has surely more of a refining, even if its truth be doubted, than the above somewhat coarse account of Wolfe's fiery locks and uncouth features, which the novelist-historian has picked up somewhere, one does not know where, to insert in his well-written volume entitled *Old Quebec*.

More pathetic and affecting than all other glimpses we get of the man, in the resolute soldier with the taint of anticipated death on his face, is the one which represents him in conversation with his old schoolmate, Midshipman John Jervis, the night before his last battle. Walking the deck of one of the ships on its way down the river at the will of the tide, he took the young officer by the arm to tell him some things that were very near his heart at that fateful moment. Taking from his bosom the portrait of his affianced bride, he pressed it upon Jervis with these words: "Here, my dear fellow, give this to her, when you return, for we shall meet no more."

Before expiring on the "greensward slope" near the site where now stands the monument to his heroism, he is said to have presented his sash and pistols to the surgeon who attended him. The sash, which was one of woven crimson silk, was sadly rent and stained with blood—a sad memento of the life which is still revered by a whole empire, and one which ought to be recovered and preserved as a token of his bravery. Of him and the glorious event in which his life was sacrificed at a nation's demand, Thomas Carlyle, the historian of *Frederick the Great*, thus speaks after his own inimitable manner: "By ten of the clock, Wolfe stands ranked (just somewhat in the Frederick way, though on a small scale), ready at all points for Montcalm, but refusing to be over-ready. Montcalm, volleying and advancing, can get no response, more than from Druidic stones; till at thirty yards the stones become vocal—and continued so at a dreadful rate; and, in the space of seven minutes, have blown Montcalm's regulars, and their second in command, and their third in command too, into ruin and destruction. In about seven minutes more, the French army was done for, the English falling on with bayonets and the Highlanders with claymore; then fierce pursuit, rout total— and Quebec and Canada as good as finished. The thing is yet well known to Englishmen; and how Wolfe died, in it, his beautiful death."

Biography of Brigadier Monckton

THERE were three lads of about the same age who had served their apprenticeship as soldiers under the command of the Duke of Cumberland in his campaigning in Flanders and Germany, namely, James Wolfe, Robert Monckton, and George Townshend. Of these the eldest was Monckton, the second son of Viscount Galway; and, disappointing as it is, we seem to know even less of his boyhood and early education than of the others, little as that is. His mother was a daughter of the Duke of Rutland; and, sprung from such parentage, he must have had the advantages of schooling common to boys of the English nobility, though the letters written in his own hand show how deficient he was in spelling, grammar, and caligraphy.

Indeed, the first hint we have of his personal character comes from that rather unreliable critic, Horace Walpole, who tells us that "he was a very particular young man, with much address, some honour, no knowledge, great fickleness, greater want of judgment, and possessed of a disposition to ridicule, though giving promise once or twice of making a good speaker." He had been personally acquainted with Wolfe and Townshend long before the Quebec affair. Townshend and he had been joint aides-de-camp of Lord Dunmore

137

in 1745, and there had no doubt been several opportunities of their meeting around the mess table or at the society outings in London.

Monckton was but seventeen years of age when he reached his captaincy; and on his return from the battlefields of Europe, and possibly of Scotland, he found himself elected to Parliament to represent the pocket-burgh of Pontefract, much as Townshend had been elected to represent Norfolk. Of his social or domestic experiences we know as little as of his schoolboy days; while his career as a parliamentarian was limited to a season or two only, since he was called away to Nova Scotia as a military officer, to look after the pacification of the Acadians, who, through the influence of a turbulent priest, had assumed a belligerent attitude towards the government of that colony.

When Monckton reached Halifax, he was informed what part he was expected to take in the fourfold scheme propounded by the Duke of Newcastle, prime minister of England, and the Duke of Cumberland, commander-in-chief of the Empire, which had for its ultimate aim the driving of the French from their colonial possessions in America. According to this scheme, General Braddock was to turn his attention to Fort Duquesne; Colonel Johnson was to advance against the country round Crown Point; Governor Shirley was to lead a force against Niagara; and Monckton was to see after the taking of Fort Beausejour, as a preliminary to the besieging of Louisbourg for a second time.

But where was Fort Beausejour, and where were the troops with which the place was to be taken? These were the two questions which the intrepid colonel had to face. And he very soon learned that Beausejour was a compactly built stronghold—as solidly built on military principles as were the outworks of Louisbourg, situated at the head of the Bay of Fundy, on the Isthmus of Chignecto, and that there was no sufficient body of troops at hand to warrant his going against it with much prospect of success, even with Fort Lawrence near by as a centre of operations.

The first thing Monckton had to do, therefore, was to proceed to Boston to raise supplementary troops. Thence he carried a letter with him from Governor Lawrence of Nova Scotia, to Governor Shirley of Massachusetts, telling him what was going on among the Acadians, even in times of peace and English forbearance, and that the French had it no doubt in mind to repair the fortifications of Louisbourg as a preliminary to making a descent on Fort Lawrence. The issue of Monckton's visit to Boston was his return to Nova Scotia with two thousand colonial troops to take part with the British regulars in carrying out his share in the fourfold plan of the Duke of Newcastle and his royal commander-in-chief. And from the manner in which he fulfilled his duty, we readily discover how far Horace Walpole made but a poor estimate of Robert Monckton's character when he set him down as a man of no knowledge and wanting in judgment.

There was a man, however, in charge of Beausejour, who had neither knowledge nor right judgment, nor any very large measure of moral sense either. That man was Captain Verger, who afterwards was found asleep at his post the morning of the Battle of the Plains, and whose intimacy with the notorious François Bigot is referred to elsewhere in this volume. There had been a rallying around the place on the part of the Acadians before Monckton reached it. The fort was garrisoned with over one hundred and fifty men, while about twelve hundred volunteers had encamped between the fort and the little River Missiquash. Monckton had no difficulty in bridging the stream, or in taking up a commanding position a mile or so north of the fort and on the same ridge, where he was able to have two mortars directed against the place while awaiting events.

For all of four days there was an exchange of firing, interrupted by a sally on the part of the besieged, which ended only in ridicule of the leader of it. At length, what the French called their "bomb-proofs" gave way under the destructive force of Monckton's shells; and the crowding occupants of the fort—garrison soldiers and peasant volunteers, over thirteen hundred of them in all, huddling in confusion within the walls—began to clamour for some kind of escape from the dangers around them. And, when word was brought in, that the besieged need look for no succour from Louisbourg or Quebec, the confusion became a panic, until, all objection on the part of the priest who had been the cause of all the trouble having been subdued, a flag of truce was raised from the ramparts inviting negotiations for release. After some little demurring on the part of the besieged, on account of their terms being set aside by Monckton, who substituted others of his own almost as lenient, the place was evacuated, and had its name changed from Beausejour to Fort Cumberland, in honour of the Duke of Cumberland. The names of General Amherst and Colonel Monckton himself are still perpetuated in the nearest largest towns at the head of the Bay of Fundy.

In the years that followed, up to the capture of Louisbourg by Amherst and Wolfe, no one had brought home to him more directly the inconsistencies of the Acadian question than Colonel Monckton. Not even John Winslow of Boston, who had the supervision of his New England troop around the Minas Basin, knew the mind of the Council at Halifax as intimately as he did. He was not a member of that Council; and, when it was decreed that the Acadians should be expatriated, he had merely to obey as a soldier in command. Even when he was ordered to seize all the adult male Acadians in the neighbourhood of Fort Cumberland, and hold them as prisoners within its walls, and knew only too well the suffering the seizure involved for all concerned, he had nothing to do but carry out his instructions, at the demands of duty.

He was the first to inform John Winslow, as a superior officer telling his second in command, of what the two of them would have to do, irrespective of their own personal feelings in the matter. In a short time there had been gathered into the fort over four hundred of these unfortunates, awaiting the doom of their exile; though in the colonel's treatment of them there is nothing discoverable of any harshness on his part, beyond what his duty impelled him to inflict, incidental, to the decree of the Council. Indeed, the following incident may be taken as an indication that he was far from being personally sympathetic with the movement.

One day Winslow had come from Minas Bay, and was marching a body of his men past Fort Cumberland. There had been friction between the regulars and the colonial troops, much as there was jealousy against Montcalm's French soldiery on the part of the Canadian volunteers, when the former came out from France with him. The British officers had the name of being supercilious towards the Boston men; and the incident in question seems to bear out the accusation at first sight, even against Monckton himself. Winslow, it appears, had sent forward three hundred of his colonials under his second in command; and, as this officer was conducting his troop past the fort with drums beating and colours flying, Monckton sent word to him that the banners of the company should be left with the regiment, while he was out merely on the search for more Acadians to arrest and not to fight.

When Winslow heard of the peremptory order, he was very angry, and made reply to Monckton that nothing could be more uncivil and ill-natured than such treatment.

"The affair looks odd,' said the New England officer, "and will appear so in history."

But if Monckton's duty impelled him to collect the early settlers of Nova Scotia for transportation, it also forbade him to overlook a breach of military etiquette even in one so prominent in the carrying out of the expatriation scheme as John Winslow of Boston.

Around Fort Cumberland, Monckton is said to have had less success, in the gathering-in process, than the same Winslow, which perhaps may be taken as another evidence that his heart was not in such a work.

It would seem that Monckton's duties around the Isthmus prevented him from taking part under Amherst at the siege of Louisbourg; and it must have been galling to his proud spirit to be sent, when that glori-

ous event was over, down the Bay of Fundy and up
the St. John River, under orders to lose no time in
"destroying the vermin" to be found in the settlements of that district. And no more is there heard
of his doings in Nova Scotia, after that inglorious raid.

After being freed from his duties in Acadia, he must
have returned for a short season to England, where
Wolfe was also to be found after he had finished his
raid among the settlements of Northumberland Straits.
The fourfold plan of securing North America entirely
as a dependency of Great Britain directed all eyes
towards Quebec, and away from Louisbourg, which
had fallen never again to be fortified as a stronghold
either by the French or the British. And it must
have been during his stay in England that Monckton
received orders to accompany General Wolfe as his
premier brigadier-general. Whether Wolfe was entrusted with the selection of his own brigadier-generals
or not, there is no doubt that Monckton had recommended himself, as a soldier of ability and endurance,
to the War Office as well as to Wolfe. His experience
among the Acadians and their manner of warfare would
be of special service, it could not but be thought, in
dealing with the Canadians under the command of
Montcalm. He had at least the honour of being the
first to lead his men up the steep pathway of what
is now known as Wolfe's Cove, and to command the
centre, when once Wolfe had marshalled his three
divisions on the Plains of Abraham.

The five regiments which were under Monckton's
immediate charge on the 13th of September, 1759,
were the Amhersts (15th Foot); the Kennedys (43rd);
the Anstruthers (58th); the Lascelles (47th); and the

Fraser Highlanders (78th). Immediately on the second volley being fired all along the line, while he was marching at the head of the Lascelles, Monckton was wounded in the breast, the bullet entering his right lung; and when the engagement was over he was borne to his tent in Levis, with some others of the staff, who had also been disabled. One of his first orders, as first in command, was that the soldiers should put on the badge of mourning for their dead general. He had to remain in the doctor's hands, however, while Townshend and Saunders were arranging the terms of capitulation with De Ramézay and his French associates within the walls. He was too seriously injured to be disturbed with any consultation. But his rugged body and buoyant spirits soon asserted themselves, and before Townshend left for England, he was able to inform him in his own handwriting, that his health was improving, and that he had been looking over their late general's papers to find that there was nothing of any importance to transmit from them to England.

Before Saunders sailed in October, following the frigate which bore the embalmed remains of Wolfe, Monckton had made further recovery, but felt that it would be impossible for him to assume the active duties of first in command at Quebec during the winter. He therefore left Quebec before navigation closed on sick leave, and had the good fortune to join Admiral Rodney on his way to Martinique, in his famous raid upon that island in 1761. On his return he was entrusted with the position of commander-in-chief and governor of New York, from which he was recalled to England in 1763, to be rewarded with the sinecure for life of governor of Berwick and Holy Island, much as his comrade Townshend was subsequently awarded the governorship of Jersey.

From the position of ensign he had climbed all the way to be a lieutenant-general, dying in his fifty-sixth year—the hero of a hundred fights, in none of which he had ever tarnished his reputation as a valiant, skilful officer, amiable in his disposition and stable in his friendships. The artists who have left their impressions of him on the canvas, represent him as a strong, sturdy kind of a man, with leadership in his pose of body and in the lineaments of his rugged, impressive Scottish face, with features betraying persistency rather than originality of purpose, and expressing in their *tout ensemble* the will to stay by the call of duty to the minutest detail of action.

Biography of Brigadier Townshend

THE career of General George Townshend, the first Marquis of Townshend, and eldest son of the third Viscount Townshend, has to be viewed from two aspects, the military and the political, and the story of his life is not complete without following it to its close, when he died full of honours, that were induced as much through his parliamentary influence as from his prowess in the battlefield. Like Wolfe, he had his first baptism of fire on his way to the battlefield of Dettingen, which takes rank in importance with the battle of Fontenoy, where Wolfe also took part as an officer, while sharing in the momentous events of the Seven Years' War. The country-seat of the Townshend family was Raynham Hall, in Norfolk, where the subject of this sketch was born in 1724, and where he was coached to enter St. John's College, Cambridge, no doubt by the same tutor who looked after the schooling of his three brothers, Charles, Roger, and Edward. George Townshend took the full Arts course at his university, completing it with the degree of M.A.; and no sooner had he turned his back on his collegiate days, than he was seized with the martial fervour of the times, and volunteered as a soldier in the campaigns in Scotland and on the continent, though not altogether with the approval of his father. He took his first lesson in

147

campaigning as aide-de-camp to the Duke of Cumberland. Subsequently with the Duke of Newcastle, his uncle, to plead his cause with Lord Dunmore, he was appointed to a position on the staff of the army that was on the point of setting out for Flanders, with the king himself in command, the cost of his outfit being anything but pleasing to his father, the Viscount, who had to pay over four thousand dollars for it.

From his own journal, we get hints as to what manner of a young man he was. George Townshend was an aristocrat, and as such he was gifted with the eye of a proud soldier as well as a keen one, taking in all that was going on from company to battalion, even to the inner circle of the field council—learning his trade in action, as was the case in those days, with no military school for the training of cadets as there is now. From the glimpses we have of his behaviour during this early period in his career, he seems to have been guided, as were Wolfe and Montcalm in their young days, by a "whole duty of man" of his own, promoting within him a high sense of honour as a gentleman and a keen sense of duty as a soldier. At the battle of Dettingen, he was stationed by chance near the person of the king, whose courage under a severe cannonade from the enemy, as he says, gave him the opportunity of learning by example what a soldier should never forget, that, in an engagement, he is only part of a whole.

In one of his letters to Raynham Hall, this "part of a whole," however, did not fail to comment pretty severely about certain deficiencies in the conduct of the war, and his criticisms show that he was well out of his novitiate as a soldier, much as Wolfe had been, before he had reached his twentieth year:

"To give you my opinion in the most tender manner of this campaign and the conclusion of it, I consider the situation of our armies and the temper of those who conduct them to be what all seem to agree them to be, in the verdict Inglorious. I could give such an account of the declining condition of our army as would make the most indifferent person weep."

In the same way he had strictures to make in private over the field arrangements on the part of the English in the battle of Fontenoy, which took place two years after Dettingen. The youthful officer was in training to weigh the outcome—the issue of right movements and mistaken movements—as a general would do. And this his superiors knew so well that he was raised to a captaincy in Bligh's Regiment, with the approval of the Duke of Cumberland, even before he had finished his twenty-first year.

And as on the continent, so in Scotland, the young Townshend made his mark. He was present at the battle of Culloden, and afterwards at the battle of Laffelt in Flanders. In both engagements he was to be found in the very thick of the strife, and when all was over at Laffelt, he was selected by the Duke to carry home the despatches announcing the result of the bitter contest. And in this case again his spirit of criticism, or aristocratic air of fault-finding, took to task, though only privately in his own journal, the stupidity which had led to the defeat, and the prudence which had saved the British soldiery on their retreat, under General Ligonier.

On his return to England, with the Duke's unsavoury despatches to deliver, he found that during his absence he had been elected to Parliament, as member for the

county of Norfolk. Thus was his career as a politician
brought in a parallel line with his career as a soldier.
His election, however, did not obviate his return to
the seat of war, where he arrived duly gazetted as a
lieutenant-colonel, though ostensibly only in command
of a company in the Foot Guards. His critical eye
continued open, even more than ever, to the deficiencies of discipline and equipment to be met with in his
environment. In fact, he writes to his father with ill-
concealed scorn at the shortcomings of his fellow-
officers and their men, declaring that when peace came,
Britain would have to discharge a number of men from
her service whom no other European nation would
care to give soldierly employment to.

When the war came to an end, Townshend continued in charge of his regiment stationed in London,
blending his parliamentary duties with the routine
of barracks life, and taking his share in the social world
around him. In his twenty-seventh year he married
the daughter and heiress of the Earl of Northampton,
taking up his residence at Cranmer Hall, three miles
or so from the home of his boyhood. An ideal home
was Cranmer Hall, to which he brought his bride,
and where a family of two sons and a daughter were
born to him. It was not until after the death of his
father, and three years before the death of Baroness
de Ferrars, his first wife, that he moved to Raynham
Hall, where there was born to him a family of six
children by his second wife.

The first important parliamentary measure with which
Townshend was identified, was the famous Militia
Bill of 1757. There was strong opposition to the Bill
on the part of the king, as well as the king's ministry,

and even Townshend's own father was openly opposed to it.   It passed the Commons, but at first was thrown out by the House of Lords.   All the while Townshend the younger kept fighting for it as if it were a prize to be gained on the battlefield.   Finally it passed both Houses in an amended form, and received the royal assent.   But there was no end to the enemies the strife stirred up against the prime mover in the passing of the measure.   These enemies could not hinder him from organizing under the new Act a militia for the county of Norfolk, but they could watch him in the performance of his duties as a colonel in the army. In a short time, after the Act had been in force and other counties were being encouraged to follow the example of his county, Townshend was placed under arrest one day, on the pretence that he had been guilty of a breach of discipline by going to join in a hunting excursion without a formally granted leave of absence—a breach of discipline that had never before been looked upon as a very serious thing for any officer to commit during times of peace.   "There is nothing for it," remarked the discredited colonel, with his mind made up to relieve himself from an intended insult, "I am a marked man, I suppose, and therefore must resign my commission."

William Pitt, afterwards Lord Chatham, came into office for the second time with the portfolio of Secretary of State in his keeping, in 1758.   Roger Townshend, the third of the Townshend boys, had been with Amherst and Wolfe at Louisbourg.   The Duke of Cumberland was no longer commander-in-chief— he whom George's younger brother, Charles Townshend, the distinguished statesman and eloquent parliamentarian, second of the family, calls in a letter to his mother, "George's formidable and abdicated enemy." And since there was a close political alliance between Pitt and the Townshends, and Colonel George had never given up the idea of re-joining the army, it was soon arranged that he should have his commission restored to him. At length the news was carried out to Raynham, where Townshend was living for the time being, that he had been appointed to command a brigade under General Wolfe, who had been ordered to Quebec. And what an interesting moment it is, when one comes to read how these two distinguished soldiers exchanged greetings, when they learned of the new relationship between them!

"Your name was mentioned to me by the Mareschal," wrote Wolfe to Townshend on the latter's appointment, "and my answer was, that such an example in a person of your rank and character could not but have the best effects upon the troops in America, and, indeed, upon the whole military part of the nation; and I took the freedom to add that what might be wanting in experience was amply made up, in an extent of capacity and activity of mind, that would find nothing difficult in our business. I am to thank you for the good opinion you have entertained of me, and for the manner in which you have taken to express your favourable sentiments. I persuade myself, that we shall concur heartily for the public service—the operation in question requiring our united efforts and the utmost exertion of every man's spirit and judgment."

And when James Wolfe had been relieved from his bodily sickness by the bullets of the enemy, this is how his companion in arms spoke of him in the hearing of the Empire:

"I am not ashamed to own to you, that my heart does not exult in the midst of this success. I have lost but a friend in General Wolfe. Our country has lost a sure support and a perpetual honour. If the world were sensible at how dear a price we purchased Quebec in his death, it would damp the general joy. Our best consolation is that Providence seemed not to promise that he should remain long with us. He was himself sensible of the weakness of his constitution, and determined to crowd into a few years actions that would have adorned length of life."

The dispute about the change in the line of attack on Quebec is not a dispute that has any historic importance about it. Townshend was in no sense superior to Wolfe as a general. The council of war which decided that the British army should find some other way to the walls of Quebec than by way of Beauport, or beyond Cap Rouge, consisted of Wolfe, Monckton, Townshend and Murray. The decision of these men formed a consensus, and Wolfe, however sick at the time, gave his adhesion as general-in-chief to that consensus. Warburton is unfair to Wolfe just as Parkman is unfair to Townshend, in their general estimate of character from one event.

When Wolfe fell, Townshend was far afield with his division. Monckton, second in command, had also been disabled about the same time. The command-in-chief fell to Townshend, and to him and Murray falls the honour, with the co-operation of Admiral Saunders, of forcing the capitulation of the town, five days after the Battle of the Plains. Every movement of the divisions of the British army, after the death of General Wolfe, was directed by Townshend, however the story continues to be told by the various raconteurs of the event. Townshend has told us, in his letter to Pitt, that the engagement was virtually over when he was told that Wolfe had been killed. He had hardly reached the centre, which had been under the command of Monckton until he also had been disabled, for the purpose of bringing the troops into something like order, when he was informed that Bougainville was near at hand with two thousand men, who had been hastened on their march from Cap Rouge; and some of our historiographers still continue to ask why he did not at once put an end to Bougainville and his force, while others ask why Bougainville did not arrive sooner to the assistance of Montcalm.

"You will agree, sir, I flatter myself," says Townshend, writing to Pitt about the memorable event, "that it was not my business to risk the fruits of so glorious a day, and to abandon so commanding a situation, to give a fresh enemy battle upon his own terms, and in the midst of woods and swamps where he was posted." And there speaks the judicious general the final word in the controversy.

It is hardly necessary to say that George Townshend's political adversaries had no proper insight into his character as a soldier. Their party bias stood in the way of their knowing him, beyond his being an aristocrat who had beaten them in the passing of the Militia Bill. And they were soon found maintaining, in a virulent newspaper controversy, that he had been guilty of defaming the tactics of his general, of seeking to steal more than his share of the glory of the victory, and of deserting his post when he appointed Murray to remain in garrison at Quebec, instead of remaining there himself. On the score of his desertion there is no more ground for the accusation than for the other allegations. In his letter to General Amherst, when he heard that the latter was on the Richelieu, General Townshend candidly tells him why he had made up his mind to return to England.

"General Monckton," he says, "who is so well recovered as to command us again (Monckton, it must be remembered, was next in command to Wolfe at Quebec), will, I conclude, write to you upon the intelligence of the situation....and how far things may admit or not of any further movement on our side. This is not my province. He proposes to leave General Murray commander at Quebec. I cannot, consequently, whenever the army becomes a garrison, be of any use here, and may embrace the leave to return to England you so long bestowed upon me....I shall be one of the very many who shall think himself happy to serve under your command."

And the letters extant from his brother officers prove that the thought that he was deserting his post had never entered their heads, by way of suspicion even.

"You are one of the last men in the world," says Monckton in one of his letters, "that could give me offence. In regard to your going home, you will just choose your own time . . . . I hope malicious tongues will not be suffered to hurt me in your opinion."

Yet the malicious tongues of his political enemies did pursue Townshend in the most malevolent way, when he once had landed in England. One of the newspaper articles was so scurrilously sarcastic. that it was imputed for a time to the back-biting Junius. In a letter to his wife, dated September 6th, Townshend does put on a poor mouth about the conditions at Quebec, but General Wolfe had done the same in some of his letters to the War Office, insomuch that many in England were looking for a repulse rather than a victory.

Besides, Townshend had always been given to criti-- cizing in his lofty, aristocratic way, by putting himself in the general's shoes, no matter who the general was. It was in this way that he had first learned the art of war; and when he tells his wife that "General Wolfe's health is very bad, and in my opinion his generalship is not a bit better," one need not make too much of it, especially in view of what he said in his report already quoted, about the hero of the day. Townshend's latest biographer, a kinsman of his by descent, could hardly have calculated the harm he was likely to do to a brave soldier's memory, by re-publishing the vile ephemeral animadversions which once appeared in the *Advertiser* against him, with the plea of partizanship between every line of them. The answer to all that kind of thing was in the fact that he was honoured, on his return, with Admiral Saunders, by receiving the thanks of Parliament. Yet the feeling of Townshend in turn was so intense against his traducers, that he challenged Lord Albemarle to a duel over the affair, whom he suspected of having something to do with them. Many years afterwards he did fight a duel with Lord Bellemont, whom he wounded all but fatally; and it was just as well that his proposed duel with Albemarle was interrupted by his friends, or the high-spirited Townshend might have had more to answer for than being justly angry at his many detractors.

In 1761, George Townshend, now a major-general, took part in the battle of Vellinghausen, wherein Prince Ferdinand of Brunswick fought with the French against their demands in Westphalia. Next year he was ordered to Portugal in command of a division in the Anglo-Portuguese army. His brother Charles was by this time Secretary for War, and the details of this, the final campaign in the Seven Years' War, are ready of access in the letters which passed between the brothers. A reply to George's enemies, accusing him of mercenary motives in the Quebec campaign, is given in his refusal to accept pay from the Portuguese government for his services.

In 1767, he succeeded to the family estates, as fourth Viscount Townshend, and in the same year was appointed Lord-Lieutenant of Ireland. While conscientiously dealing with the usual problems of that country, he was again subjected to the full force and flippancy of the political pamphleteers. His endeavours to retain a personal popularity in spite of this, involved him in heavy expenses out of all proportion to his emoluments. His wife died during the term of his viceroyalty, and when he returned to England he was obliged to sell some of the family estates to meet his liabilities. This was, however, partly made up to him by his appointments and the honours conferred upon him on his return. In 1787, he was raised two steps in the peerage, and as Marquis of Townshend was given the rank of Field Marshal, and the sinecure of Governor of Jersey. He died in 1807, and this is how the *Gentleman's Magazine* writes of him at the close of his eventful eighty-three years:

11

"In his private life he was lively, unaffected, convivial. He possessed an acute mind, and enlivened his conversation with that original pleasantry which is shown very visibly in the works of his pencil when he chose to display it. In the early part of his life he frequently indulged in its humours, and was an admirable caricaturist, even at the time when Hogarth flourished. He suffered, indeed, some heavy afflictions, but he bore them with resignation; and closed a life, protracted beyond the common date of man, with the general respect and estimation of his country."

There is a hint in the above panegyric which reminds us that the age in which Wolfe and Townshend and Monckton were in the public eye was the age of Hogarth and Horace Walpole, as well as of Junius and his brother pamphleteers. It was an age in which critical coarseness and caricature took the place of refinement of wit and literary forbearance—the age in which Warren Hastings, soldier and statesman, was made to suffer the torments of the gridiron in all its unsympathetic phases. Nor did George Townshend's character escape being marred by the manners of the times. Some of his jokes savoured of the Duke of Cumberland kind; as, for instance, when a soldier near him in the battlefield had his head blown off, he is reported as having callously remarked that he had not known, till then, what a quantity of brains the poor victim had possessed. And the story of his having passed round the mess table a pencilled caricature of General Wolfe, while the great main problem of taking Quebec was imminent, is in keeping with some of the social influences of his day. There is no hiding of the fact that Townshend was a fault-finder, and as such he was not infrequently found infringing upon the "whole duty of man" he had laid down for his guidance as a Christian gentleman.

The portraitures of him which have been handed down represent him as a man of prepossessing presence in every line of his pose. His features were clean-cut and regular, with a mouth indicative of firmness and eyes possessing a twinkle in them of merriment or a flash of sarcasm, as the spirit behind them happened to be moved. The aristocratic look in such a face might be taken to indicate that there was some truth in what his enemies have said about his supercilious demeanour towards even his superiors, but there is in it no corroboration of what they have said of his lack of courage or incapacity. He was a man of the times, seldom disinclined to pay back in the open his Roland for an Oliver, and even sometimes suspecting inferiority in others when there was no room for such suspicion.

Biography of General Murray

GENERAL JAMES MURRAY, son of a Scottish nobleman, was but a young man when he was ordered out
to Canada as one of General Wolfe's three brigadiers.
Previous to this, he had seen service on the continent
of Europe, notably with the Duke of Cumberland at
the battle of Fontenoy, in 1745. As we know, he
had charge of the right centre at the Battle of the
Plains; and, in the re-arrangements of army appointments after the contest, he was left in charge of the
captured town. Under the condition of affairs that
beset him, with a mixed population to deal with, and
with every branch of industry in disorder in a community that had to be re-organized *ab fundamento*—
he could hardly miss being misunderstood, even by his
own soldiers. The misadventure of his opposing a
force twice his own in numbers in the battle of Sainte-
Foye, gave rise for a time to many misgivings at Quebec and in England concerning his discretion; though
now it has been clearly proven to have been only a
selection on his part of the least of two evils. "When
I considered that our little army," he wrote to Pitt,
"was in the habit of beating that enemy, and had a
very fine train of field artillery; and that shutting ourselves at once within the walls was putting all upon
the single, chance of holding out for a considerable
161

time a wretched fortification, I resolved to give them
battle; and, half an hour after six in the morning, we
marched with all the force I could muster, namely,
three thousand men."

Quebec was in no condition to withstand a siege by
De Lévis any more than it had been to hold out against
the British six months previously. And relying on
the bravery and staying powers of his men, Murray
thought it his duty to take chances on his breaking up
his adversary's large and mixed army at one blow.
He failed; but failure is not always blameworthy, however prone the unthinking be to judge it so. And, if
the efforts that were once made to discredit his foresight as a soldier were repeated to discredit him as a
governor, we now know that he was not only a gallant
soldier, but one who was upright, humane and generous
in his dealings with friend and foe. Though placed
between two stools, the "vanquished and the victors"
in his administration of affairs, in no instance can he
be said to have wavered in his integrity, by pitting
his one means of support against the other, as is too
often done while dealing with two parties in one juris-
diction, such as his was as first English governor in
Canada. The most uncomfortable feature in his administration was the distrust he met so often in his
endeavours to establish a safe *in medias res*. Yet no
injustice of opinion could divert him from his steadfast
line of duty; and this is now his highest credit, when
we bring ourselves to judge of his character without
racial or religious bias.

The capitulation of the city of Quebec took place a
full year before the capitulation of Montreal and the
whole country; and hence General Murray had to put

things to right as best he could in his own neighbourhood, before there was peace in the parishes and the
smaller towns.   And this setting things to right included
the housing of his troops in proper quarters under
military oversight and discipline, the renewing of the
dwellings for all those depending on the army for
support, the providing for regular markets, and the
ridding of the town of the sick by housing them in the
General Hospital, or by sending them *en hôpital* to
the Island of Orleans, where an atmosphere clear of
the lingering scents of war and catastrophe would
tend to their speedier recovery.

Captain John Knox, in his diary, tells how he himself managed to make himself comfortable in a stable
with a few sticks of furniture, and what a relief it was
for the soldiers to be taken from their dog-holes in the
barracks hospital, to be placed under the care of the
nuns.   And from the same source we learn further
of the state of things during that first winter after
the siege.

And hardly had Murray brought the town into some
kind of order, when he was instructed by General
Amherst to join him at Montreal with as large a detachment as he could, with safety to Quebec, bring with
him: The removal of this contingent was afterwards
made up for, by the arrival of two regiments from
Louisbourg, thus enabling Murray to set out on his
march with few misgivings.

The purpose of that journey up the river and along
the parish roads near it, was to prepare the inhabitants for a peaceful acceptance of their new masters.
And its record, covering all of a five weeks' march, is
but part of the story of the final surrender of Governor

Vaudreuil, and need not be narrated here. An incident that occurred at the very moment of the signing of the terms of capitulation is, however, worthy of mention, as illustrative of the high integrity and resoluteness of Murray's character, as is another incident, which occurred while he was Governor of Minorca several years afterwards.

After retiring from Canada, Murray was appointed to the governorship of the second largest of the Balearic Islands in the Mediterranean. While there, the island was invested by the combined fleets of France and Spain, under the command of Duc de Crillon; but when the military skill of Murray had brought the invaders to the point of despair, the Duc de Crillon sought to bribe the brave defender. This was in 1781. And the bribe was no small affair, either. By it James Murray, the first Governor of Canada, had a chance of becoming a millionaire, for the bribe offered for the surrender of Minorca was no less a sum than one million pounds sterling, or five million dollars. The scorn with which the offer was rejected was instant and decisive. "I can have no further communication with you but in arms," answered the angry Murray. "If you send clothing for your unfortunate prisoners in my possession, leave it at a distance to be taken up for them, because I will admit of no contact for the present, but such as is hostile to the most inveterate degree."

And the incident at the time of the capitulation of Montreal was no less an illustration of the man's resoluteness. While the negotiations were in progress Amherst had sent to Murray for some information relative to the state of affairs at Quebec, as an elucidation of a point in question between the negotiators. Murray at once sent one of his officers to give the information by word of mouth. As that officer was passing round the walls of the fort on his errand, he was seized upon by some of Bourlamaque's men and placed in custody. Next day, when Murray learned what had happened to his messenger, he marched up to Bourlamaque's quarters with a body of soldiers, and demanded the liberation of the prisoner. Bourlamaque came out to confer in person, but refused the release of his prisoner. "Then I give you five minutes to undo an injustice!" exclaimed Murray, as he gave orders for the advance of one or two of his largest guns. What would have happened can only be surmised, from what happened in the case of the Duc de Crillon afterwards, if word had not at that moment been brought to the angry General that the terms of capitulation had been agreed upon.

On Murray's memorable trip up the river from parish to parish, he seems to have won golden opinions alike from *seigneur* and *habitant*. His capacity for dealing with people possessed of a prejudice was amazing. One French-Canadian ventured to tell his compatriots that General Murray had done more harm to the so-called "Canadian Party" by his policy as governor than by his army. "He stopped often in the villages; spoke kindly to the inhabitants he found at home in their houses—whom hunger and famine had obliged to fly from our army in Montreal; gave provisions to those unhappy creatures perishing for want of subsistence...In short, flattering some and frightening others, he succeeded so well that at last there was no possibility of keeping their neighbours at

Montreal, when once they heard from the others what his policy was."

The first government under British auspices was necessarily military. General Murray should therefore not be ranked as a civil administrator, during his first year or two of rule. He was only one of three officers in the colony, there being three districts to be supervised, namely, Quebec, Three Rivers, and Montreal. General Murray was military overseer at Quebec, Colonel Burton at Three Rivers, and General Gage at Montreal. And there was plenty of overseeing for all of them, considering the unsettled condition of the country; for it required a firm hand to keep in check the animosities between what were called "the new subjects" and "the old subjects" of the king of Great Britain in Canada—the former consisting of the returning French-Canadians, and the latter for the most part consisting of transient traders, mechanics, half-pay officers, and disbanded soldiers.

One special act of Murray's was one which the so-called new subjects would not forgive, and that was the turning of the Jesuits' College into a military barracks. Being a local question, the storm was of the violence of boiling water in a tea-kettle. The offence was a sacrilege within a sacrilege, the French religionists maintained, since Protestant worship was allowed within its walls. But in time, the soldier-governor showed that he was no bigot, but had it in mind to govern impartially all who proved themselves loyal to the new order of things.

The repudiation of the debts of the colony, incurred by Bigot and his gang of grafters, was a serious matter from the standpoint of many of the well-to-do French-

Canadian citizens, who had been deceived into invest-
ing their all in these scoundrels' boodling schemes; and
one of Murray's main difficulties was the scarcity of
money, without which, as he felt, there could be no
assurance in civic or social relations. Some have said
that the difficulties which beset the governor would
have been materially obviated had there not been so
much haste in introducing English law and the English language among those who could not but look upon
the change of masters, that had been forced upon them,
as more or less of a disgrace; and this has been to some
extent advanced as a grievance whenever reference is
made to the unpopularity of subsequent governors
who have sanctioned the suspension of the laws, language, and customs of the French regime. After the
signing of the Treaty of Paris in 1763, the King of
England issued a proclamation, according to which
it pleased him to divide up the lands which had been
decreed to him, into three provinces, namely, Quebec,
East Florida, and Grenada. The British province of
Quebec thus established had about the same territorial
limits which the Dominion of Canada has to-day; and
over it, as its first governor, political and military,
General James Murray was immediately appointed.

Murray's first effort was to induce an immigration
policy, whereby all that was required of any new settler was an avowed allegiance to the king of Great
Britain and obedience to the laws of the land. The
property taken up by this class of settlers was to be
held in free and common soccage, entirely optional as
to seignorial obligations. And under this new policy
many of the disbanded soldiers took unto themselves
Canadian wives, and settled down to the life of the

farmer. The settlement of Murray Bay bears the impress to the present day of the advice as well as the name of the general who suggested the change.

And another of Murray's tasks as governor was to organize courts for the formal administration of justice, outside of all court-martial procedure. As there was a Supreme Council organized, so was there a Supreme Court of Justice arranged for, with subordinate courts presided over by Justices of the Peace, as well as properly constituted police supervision in the various parishes. And yet, notwithstanding all the precautions the astute soldier-magistrate took to meet the necessities of the case in an impartial way, his government did not escape being denounced by new subjects and old subjects as one more arbitrary than the military rule which had preceded it, notwithstanding that it was not empowered to impose taxes on them.

It was during Governor Murray's tenure of office there occurred the Indian War which has gone down in history as the Conspiracy of Pontiac. Towards the close of his term, the General had almost as many serious problems of administration to face, as in the earlier days of it. One of these was the allaying of the storm over the proclamation that the criminal laws of England, with trial by jury, should be recognized in Canada. For a time there was no allaying of it, since he found himself placed upon the rack between two ethical prejudices that would not be appeased—the one opposed to the granting of anything that looked like a privilege to the French-Canadians, and the other siding with the idea that, to save the situation, it was necessary to temper justice with an easy philanthropy, since even the conquered had rights to be respected. It is doubtful whether any man or governor could have kept the balance of these prejudices so long on a safe swing as did the soldier-administrator. At last he was virulently accused of partiality by those of his own nationality. He favoured the French-Canadians, it was claimed, to the compromising of English interests. And at last certain English residents went so far as to lay their grievances at the foot of the throne. To meet the charges of his accusers, Murray asked for leave of absence, in order that he might plead his cause in England in his own person. Eventually there was found to be nothing substantial in any of the charges against his administration of affairs. He was completely exonerated of all blame; yet, as often occurs in such cases, it was deemed prudent to provide for him a place in the army again, and allow Sir Guy Carleton to take his position out in Canada.

It is worthy of note, in its local interest, that General Murray had his residence on the very scene of the battle he had lost to General de Lévis, at least during the later years of his administration. Out on the Ste. Foye Road these names still linger, namely, Belmont, Sans Bruit Farm, and Holland House. All of these properties are said to have belonged to him at one time; at least we are told that General Montgomery in 1775 took possession of General Murray's house when he paid his memorable visit to Quebec, for the purpose of taking possession of the whole city, with the assistance of Benedict Arnold.

General Murray died in England in 1794, and Dr. Henry Morgan, in his "Canadian Celebrities," strikes a just estimate of his character in these words: "He ended a long career in the service of his country, in which he had risen to high distinction. As a soldier, he stood foremost in the army, and had won his promotions by his own merit and his own good sword, owing nothing to influence. As a genuine Christian officer, he was esteemed by all good men, and ever distinguished for his humanity and readiness to relieve the oppressed."

A legend is told of him, that on his body being opened after death there were found in it several bullets by which he had been wounded on the battlefields of his country; and one pauses to wonder how many wounds he was called upon to count, during his lifetime, that had been inflicted on his honesty of purpose, as he strove to deal impartially with those who failed to understand it.

General Murray's physical appearance has not been flattered by those who have sent his picture down to posterity. He is represented as having had a physiognomy devoid of every trait we would expect to find in it, with a face wan and irregular of feature as of one who had been old-looking from his youth up, and with a nose and chin threatening to meet as a protection to thin and purposeless lips. General Wolfe has had his face sadly caricatured alike by historian and artist; but the face, which has been passed off as General Murray's, is the work of an artist who has left nothing for the caricaturist to work upon.

HÉBERT'S STATUE OF MONTCALM

Biography of General Montcalm

LOUIS JOSEPH DE SAINT-VERAN, Marquis de Montcalm, was a man of middle age when he received his commission from the king of France to take charge of the French and Canadian troops in New France. He was born of noble parentage, in the Chateau de Candiac, near the town of Nimes, in 1712. Before his arrival in America, and when his school days were once over, he had climbed up step by step, much as James Wolfe had done, in his advancement in the army, and, very much after the manner of his rival, through his own native ability and military skill and courage. He was in his forty-fourth year when he was brought to the notice of the king by the Minister of War, M. d'Argenson, as a fit and proper general to be sent out to Canada to take the place vacated by Baron de Dieskau, commander-in-chief under Governor-General M. de Vaudreuil. His parents were both sprung from noble lineage. While still a boy, he spent much of his time out at Roquemaure, the residence of his godmother, his own mother's grandmother; and while there, being a sickly child, he was allowed to reach his sixth year without any special schooling. His first schoolmaster was M. Louis Dumas, to whose school at Grenoble he was sent as a resident pupil; and although he made progress in his Latin and Greek, his proficiency was thrown in the shade by the precocity of his younger brother, and somewhat depreciated by his perhaps too exacting teacher.

Like Wolfe, he took up with the life of a soldier when he was only fifteen years of age; and it was as an ensign in the Regiment de Hainaut that he first saw active service at the sieges of Kehl and Philipsbourg. When he was still a subaltern, his father died, leaving him only a moderate patrimony, thus placing him, as Wolfe was placed, a soldier with only his salary to depend upon for his living. Yet, narrow as his means were, he did not draw back from marrying Angelique-Louise du Talon, daughter of the Marquis du Boulay, a colonel in the French army, and a scion of the family from which Jean Talon, the Intendant of New France, had previously sprung.

After his marriage, he continued to rise in his profession; though, during the interims of peace, he spent his time at home, with his growing family, which, by the time he became colonel, numbered two sons and four daughters. In 1743, he was placed in command of the Regiment d'Auxerrois. Thereafter he took part in sundry campaigns in Germany and Italy, attaining to the rank of brigadier-general after the disastrous battle of Piacenza, gained over the French by the Austrians, much as Wolfe had been promoted for personal valour after the failure of the British before Rochfort. During the struggle at Piacenza, Montcalm displayed the most steadfast courage, until he was dragged a prisoner from the field covered with wounds, to await an exchange of prisoners, before he could be returned to his own country.

After the Treaty of Aix-la-Chapelle, in 1748, there were times of peace in France. The Regiment d'Auxerrois was disbanded, and for a period of six years Montcalm was suffered to lead the life of a country gentleman at his Chateau de Candiac, giving special heed to the education of his eldest son, whom he intended for the army, and who was actually appointed captain of a division of the troops Montcalm was about to take with him to America. The date of Montcalm's commission as general in New France was 1756, or three years before he was called upon to meet the besiegers of Quebec on the Plains of Abraham.

When he arrived in Quebec, he had to proceed to Montreal to meet his superior, Governor Vaudreuil, for it must be kept in mind that Vaudreuil was specially mentioned in Montcalm's commission as such. The activity and military experience of the new general rallied for a time the courage of New France, the taking of Oswego and Fort William Henry being brilliant preludes to his victorious defence against the incompetent Abercrombie at Carillon, in 1758. Indeed, the story of his campaigning round the southern end of Lake Champlain, forms one of the most engrossing chapters in the annals of French soldiery in America; and his great feat at Ticonderoga may be quoted here as an illustration of the stubbornness that kept Wolfe at bay for nearly four months at Quebec.

The prelude to the repulse of the British at Carillon on the narrows between Lake Champlain and Lake George, was a disastrous one for the French. A company of Bourlamaque's division, having lost their way in the woods, had been surrounded by a full division of Abercrombie's army, and all but annihilated. The

12

situation at Carillon was different, the defence of the place being perhaps the crowning victory in Montcalm's whole career. The scene of the event and the struggle itself are thus vividly and concisely described by Andrew Archer:

"An embankment of earth, eight feet high, sloped gradually down for a hundred feet; trees were embedded in it, with their sharpened ends pointed outwards; a dreary swamp spread out before it. The country all around was covered with a close thick wood, with tangled brush and underwood. Scores upon scores of the rushing English were staked upon these pointed branches. The impetuous Highlanders tried to clamber over the barricades, and hacked furiously at them with their broadswords. In another part of the field one English regiment fired by mistake into another English regiment, killing hundreds of their brothers-in-arms, and wounding many others. A panic spread throughout the English army. The blood of the dead and dying reddened the pools of the oozy swamps; the brave besiegers had pierced their hearts upon the stakes in vain. Sheltered and almost unseen, the French met each assault with a withering fire. The Britishers finally throwing away their arms, broke into uncontrollable flight, and made for the landing-place at the side of the lake; and, but for the coolness of Colonel Bradstreet, who checked them by the levelled muskets of a few men who had retained their nonchalance, hundreds might have perished in the waters of the lake, while seeking to scramble into the boats. Nearly two thousand of the assailants fell dead and wounded in the disastrous attack. By it Abercrombie lost his character as a soldier and his command as a general."

Yet even in that moment of triumph, Montcalm was convinced that his efforts were in the way of being finally neutralized by the indifference of the home government and the spendthrift incompetency of those in charge of affairs at Quebec and Montreal. The great initial mistake lay at the door of the king of France. That monarch had sent out as his commander-in-chief in America, one who, in terms of his commission, was subject to Governor Vaudreuil in all things pertaining to the colony, and this in face of the previous recommendation of the same governor that no such an officer was needed, nor should be appointed. The condition of the colony, as Montcalm soon saw, was one almost past believing, not only from the fiscal rascalities being indulged in and winked at, but in the poverty of the people. And how there has ever come to be any closing of the eyes to the true cause of the fall of Quebec and the surrender of the whole country, is incomprehensible, with the records of the fickle-mindedness of Vaudreuil as a governor, and of the prodigalities of Bigot as an Intendant in evidence as they were and are. Indeed, when Montcalm was making ready for his last campaign to save Quebec, he is known to have indirectly prophesied in the hearing of his intimates, that it was only too likely that his own grave would be found under the ruins of the ill-fated French colony of New France.

Nor can his reverse at Quebec be properly understood without a knowledge of the relations that existed between him and Governor Vaudreuil. When Vaudreuil was thrown into the Bastile, on his arrival in Paris after the siege, the suspicions which lay at his door, it has to be said, were not charges of corruption in his own behalf, but of connivance at the barefaced acts of those whom he ought to have restrained and punished. He was liberated. But his memory can never be freed by posterity from the stain upon it, through his conduct towards Montcalm, which has already been hinted at. For instance, when Montcalm's popularity was at its zenith over the rout at the head of Lake Champlain, the peevish Vaudreuil could not keep out of sight his envy of the most distinguished French officer in Canada at the time, by blaming him for not turning the retreat of the English at Carillon into a more decisive victory. "When I go to war," was the only answer vouchsafed by the general to the jealous-minded governor, "I do the best I can; and if you are not satisfied, it might be well for you to take to the field in person yourself."

And the advocate who would think to condemn Montcalm for the unfortunate estrangement between the general and the governor, must assume the burden of justifying the discredited coterie whom Vaudreuil is known to have used as his tools to undermine Montcalm's influence even among his own men. It is now no secret that the unworthy Vaudreuil joined with the Bigot peculators to have Montcalm ousted from his command in Canada. Nay, when that open-minded soldier, M. de Bougainville, went to Paris to lay the condition of affairs in New France before the home authorities, Vaudreuil and Bigot had him traduced as a "creature of the general," who knew nothing of fiscal affairs.

And further has it become known that, failing in his importunity with the home authorities to have Montcalm removed, Vaudreuil did not fail to keep other irons in the fire for the man he envied so sorely. "The incapable and trifling Vaudreuil," says Dussiex, "counselled and incited by Bigot, converted into matters of serious complaint all the insignificant differences which were continually springing up amongst the soldiers, the militia, the savages, and the colonists. He complained bitterly of Montcalm, because it was difficult for a good understanding to subsist between his soldiers and the colonists, and because of the haughty fashion in which the latter were treated by his officers."

Nor will any one be inclined to blame Montcalm for speaking his mind freely in some of his despatches to the French War Office, over the deplorable condition of affairs in New France, even if the recital was more or less a reprisal. We now know that every word he said was true. "I have no confidence in M. Vaudreuil or in Bigot," he writes, in one of his official letters. In fact, he hints that the latter and his clientele of boodle-mongers seemed to be working for the immediate ruin of the colony, in order that their misdeeds might be covered up in the catastrophe. "It seems to me," he says, "that all out here are in haste to enrich themselves before the country is lost to France; greediness has affected every one—officers, storekeepers, clerks and others."

Nor, again, is there lack of further evidence to prove the actual fact of Vaudreuil's indirect methods of annoying Montcalm, his petty spite continuing even after the brave man's death. In a word, the awful plight into which the country had been dragged was Montcalm's chief restraint, all through his campaigning in America. He was popular with his own soldiers, but not with the mixed army as a whole. Many of the volunteers and nearly all of the *habitant* fieldsmen looked upon him with varying degrees of disfavour, being swayed in their prejudices more or less by the so-called "Canadian Party" which Bigot and his creatures had brought into being, under the auspices of Vaudreuil's bias, to suit their own purposes.

The Marquis de Montcalm was a skilful general; his genius as a commander had been proven on the battlefields of Europe, and in presence of the intrepid Highlanders at Ticonderoga. But what success is there to be looked for, from the skill of the most skilful general who, while being brought face to face with the enemy he has been specially appointed to subdue, has on the one side of him the indifference of those who have commissioned him to fight their battles, and on the other side scarcity of supplies ever imminent, and an undermining envy ever leering at him with its evil eye? These were what the brave Montcalm had to contend with, during his three years' residence in Canada, all three of them, right up to the morning when he was called upon to meet General James Wolfe on the Plains of Abraham; and well it may be asked, though sadly, what other fate could have befallen him and his brave comrades than that which did befall them under the circumstances?

And as with Wolfe, so also is it in the case of Montcalm, we can readily learn from his own letters what manner of man he was. His kindly, close-shaven face, over-topped by a peruke of modest proportions, is still to be studied from authentic portraits which have been handed down to us of him, his mellow eyes expressive of open-minded authority, and his firmly-drawn lips denoting steadfastness of purpose and amiability of temper. There is no caricaturing of such a countenance, nor misunderstanding of it either; for one can read from it the lines indicative of the loving husband, the solicitous father, the loyal servant, as well as the calculating spirit of the soldier high in command.

His "whole duty of man," as embodied in a letter to his father while he was yet a youth under the tutelage of M. Dumas at Grenoble, is one very much simpler than Wolfe's, and is perhaps one which could be read with profit by many of our youth of the present day.

"In a few words here are my aims," he says, while answering his tutor's allegations about his progress at school. "First, to be an honourable man of good morals, brave and a Christian; second, to read in moderation, and know as much Latin and Greek as most men of the world, with a knowledge of the four rules of arithmetic, and something of history, geography, and French and Latin belles-lettres, as well as to have a taste for the arts and sciences and a fondness for intellectual accuracy, even if I do not possess it myself; third, to be obedient, docile, and very submissive to your orders and those of my dear mother, and to defer to the advice of my tutor, M. Dumas; and fourth, to fence and ride as well as my small abilities will permit."

Then, again, what a homelike insight is there given to his inner character from the letter he sent to his mother, while he was taking the first steps towards preparing for setting out for Canada:

"Last night I came from Versailles, and am going back to-morrow. The king gives me twenty-five thousand francs, as he did to M. Dieskau, besides twelve thousand for my equipment, which will cost me above a thousand crowns more, but I cannot stop for that." Then again: "My affairs begin to get on. A good part of the baggage went off the day before yesterday in the king's waggons; an assistant cook and two livery men yesterday. I have a good cook. Estève, my secretary, will go on the eighth; Joseph and Déjean will follow me. To-morrow evening I go to Versailles till Sunday, and will write from there. I have three aides-de-camps; one of them Bougainville, a man of parts and pleasant company. Yesterday I presented my son, with whom I am well pleased, to the royal family."

The above to his mother and this to his wife:

"I arrived, dearest, this morning, and stay here all day. I shall be at Brest on the twenty-sixth. My son has been here since yesterday for me to coach him and get him a uniform made, in which he will give thanks for his regiment, at the same time I take leave in my embroidered coat. Perhaps I shall leave debts behind. I wait impatiently for the bills. You have my will; I wish you would have it copied and send it to me before I sail."

The incompatibility between Montcalm and Vaudreuil was something which could hardly be avoided, considering the characters of the two men. The first glimpse we have of Montcalm's opinion of the weak-minded governor is to be met with in a letter written to his friend d'Argenson, of the War Office in Paris.

"M. Vaudreuil," he says, in his laconic way, "respects the Indians, loves the Canadians, is acquainted with the country, has good sense, but is somewhat weak, and I stand very well with him."

And from it we can easily read between the lines that M. Vaudreuil, as Montcalm had detected, had from the first no very high opinion of the French. How different is what he had to say of the Marquis de Lévis, after he had met him for the first time with Bourlamaque and Bougainville, when on the point of sailing for Quebec from Brest! "I like the Chevalier de Lévis," he says, "and I think he likes me."

And the following two letters, the one from Montcalm to the French War Office, and the other from Vaudreuil, show up the disparity in their characters in a marked degree. The open-minded Montcalm all but boyishly says: "The Indians are enraptured of me, and, learning that I return to the camp at Carillon, they have been induced to march thither. The Canadians are satisfied with me; their officers esteem me, fear me, and would be well pleased could Frenchmen and their general be dispensed with, which would also gratify me. I have deemed it my duty to express myself pleased to the Keeper of the Seals, with all the colonial troops, and not to appear dissatisfied with anything."

And alongside of it comes the one from Vaudreuil, much about the same time: "M. de Montcalm has got so quick a temper that he goes so far as to strike the Canadians. I had urgently recommended him to see that the land officers treat them well; but how can he keep them in order if he cannot restrain his own vivacity? The Canadians and Indians have bitterly complained about the high-handed fashion in which M. de Montcalm dealt with them at Chouaguen."

And who is there to avoid having a kindly feeling towards one who could write to his wife and family at home in the following simple way, while he was yet in the midst of his new experiences in Canada? It tells us more of the man within him than a whole volume of fine writing could. The quotation is only one of many that could be made.

"Think of me affectionately," he writes to his wife; "give love to my girls. I hope next year to be with you all. I love you tenderly, dearest." And again: "There is not an hour in the day when I do not think of you. Out here I have to live creditably, and so I do; sixteen persons at table every day. Once a fortnight I dine with the Governor-General and with Chevalier de Lévis, who lives well too. He has given three grand balls. As for me, up to Lent I gave, besides dinners, great suppers, with ladies, three times a week. They lasted till two in the morning; and then there was dancing. It is very expensive, not very amusing, and often tedious. At Quebec, where we spent a month, I gave receptions or parties at the Intendant's house. I like my gallant Chevalier de Lévis very much. Bourlamaque was a good choice; he is steady and cool, with good parts. Bougainville has talent, a warm head and a warm heart; he will ripen in time. Write to Madame Cormier that I like her husband; he is perfectly well, and as impatient for peace as I am. Love to my daughters and all affection and respect to my mother. I live only in the hope of joining you all again. Nevertheless, Montreal is as good a place as Alais, even in time of peace, and better now, for the government is here; for the Marquis de Vaudreuil, like me, spent only a month at Quebec. As for Quebec, it is as good as the best cities of France, except ten or so. Clear sky,

bright sun; neither spring nor autumn, only summer
and winter. July, August, September, hot as in Languedoc; winter insupportable; one must keep always
indoors. The ladies *spirituelles*, *galantes*, *dévotés*.
Gambling at Quebec, dancing and conversation at Montreal. My friends the Indians, who are often unbearable, and whom I treat with perfect tranquillity and
patience, are fond of me. If I were not a sort of general, though very subordinate to the Governor, I could
gossip to you about the plans of the campaign, which
it is likely will begin on the tenth or fifteenth of May.
I worked at the plan of the last affair (Fort William
Henry), which might have turned out bett:r, though
good as it was. I wanted only eight hundred men.
If I had had my way, Chevalier de Lévis or M. de Bougainville would have had charge of it. However, the
thing was all right, and in good hands. The Governor, who is extremely civil to me, gave it to his brother;
he thought him more used to winter marches. Adieu,
my heart; I adore and love you."

The moral tone in Montcalm's manner could hardly
be pleasing to the lower moral tone that prevailed at
Quebec, while Bigot was still riding his high horse of
profligacy in the years and months before the siege.
And this letter brings a corroboration of the contrast.

"Yesterday, I spoke about retrenchment on our
tables," he notes down in his journal. "M. de Vaudreuil has approved of my views and promised to set
a good example. The whole colony praises the idea,
but the Intendant is not enthusiastic. He likes osten-
tation, and this is not the time for it. I have said
that, during the whole winter, there should be no balls,
no violins, no entertainments, no pleasure parties."

And the over-riding of the agreement between the Governor and the General by the heedless Bigot, gave the latter a chance of putting on record his opinions of Bigot's prodigal munificence in his palace. Despite the orders issued by Montcalm against gambling, the Intendant issued invitations for a large party on a certain Sunday evening, ostensibly under the announcement of its being only a concert given by the officers of the garrison. After the music, however, the tables were set for gambling, and this is the account the General has left of the after orgy in his journal:

"The gaming was so far beyond the means of the men engaged in it, that I thought I was looking on at fools, or rather at sick people with burning fever, for I do not remember seeing the stakes as high, unless at the king's game. If all these gamblers who seem to squander their money would only scrutinize their feelings, they would see that, notwithstanding their inclination to spend, this passion for gambling is the result of greed and cupidity."

And surely these words and what he after hints at in his indirect estimation of Bigot's character, cannot but convince us that the Marquis de Montcalm was not one who had swerved from the first rule of life which he laid down in his boyish days as a guidance in his conduct, namely, "My first aim is to be an honourable man of good morals, brave and a Christian."

And one more letter to his wife, the second, last perhaps he ever was permitted to write to her, may be given, to show what he meant when he told De Ramézay that he had no more to do with the affairs of state, since there was left to him only a remnant of time in which to think of his dear ones at home in France and his

God, his communion being last with the Father of All. The letter in question was written a little while before he received the news from Candiac that his eldest son and daughter were both married, and that his "dear little Minette," a younger daughter, had died.

"Can we hope for another miracle to save us?" he asks his wife. "I trust in God; He fought for us on the eighth of July. Come what may, His will be done. I wait the news from France with impatience and dread. We have had none for eight months, and who knows if much can reach us at all this year? How dearly I have to pay for the dismal privilege of figuring two or three times in the gazettes!" And the sequel to that letter is the one after he has heard again from home: "Our daughter is well married. I think I would gladly renounce every honour to be with you again; but the king must be obeyed. The moment when I see you once more will be the brightest in my life. Adieu, my heart; I believe that I love you more than ever."

The closing scene in his life has all the conceivable dismal lights of disappointment and sorrow about it. After he had vainly striven to reduce the retreat from the battlefield into some semblance of order, he entered the city by the St. Louis Gate, and as he passed down the narrow street he was met by the crowding citizens blending with the soldiers who had not made for the bridge of boats across the St. Charles.

"Oh, *mon dieu, mon dieu*, the Marquis is killed!" cried some of the women as they saw the blood dripping from his saddle; while he, holding up his hands by way of expostulating with them, quietly replied: "It is nothing, it is nothing; do not trouble yourselves about me!"

He is said to have breathed his last in the house of one of the city's physicians in Louis Street. His own house stood on the ramparts overlooking the harbour. His remains were deposited within the precincts of the Ursuline Convent. The funeral, which took place on the day of his death, is thus described by Sir James Lemoine, in his *Picturesque Quebec:*

"At nine o'clock in the evening of the 14th of September, 1759, a funeral cortege, issuing from the Castle, winds its way through the dark and obstructed streets to the little church of the Ursulines. With the heavy tread of the coffin-bearers, keeps time the measured footsteps of the military escort, De Ramézay and the other officers of the garrison following to their resting-place the lifeless remains of their illustrious commander-in-chief. No martial pomp was displayed round that humble bier, but the hero who had afforded the sublime spectacle of a Christian yielding up his soul to God in the most admirable sentiments of faith and resignation, was not laid in unconsecrated ground. No burial rite could have been more solemn than that hurried evening service performed by torchlight under the dilapidated roof of a sacred asylum, where the soil had been first laid bare by one of the rude engines of war—a bombshell. The grave tones of the priests murmuring the *Libera me Domine* were responded to by the sighs and tears of consecrated virgins, henceforth the guardians of the precious deposit, which, but for inevitable fate, would have been reserved to do honour to some proud mausoleum. With gloomy forebodings and bitter thoughts De Ramézay and his companions in arms withdrew in silence. A few citizens had gathered in, and among the rest one led by the hand his little daughter, who, looking into the grave, saw and remembered, more than three-fourths of a century later, the rough wooden box which was all the ruined city could afford to enclose the remains of her defender."

The above extract is hardly in accordance with the facts of the case, the funeral from the Chateau and the improvised grave hollowed out by cannon ball being quite unauthentic. The authorities of the Ursuline Convent have still in their keeping all that was left of Montcalm's remains when his grave—within the chapel, and not in the grounds without—was being opened for the reception of the dead body of one of the *contre-maitres* of the institution. And as with the dead body of General Murray when it was exhumed, with its many bullet wounds, so, in the case of General Montcalm's skull, there are to be traced several marks as if from sword blows he had received while fighting the battles of his country.

And what a wonderful prophecy was that of his which he made shortly before he died about the fate that was to befall the New England colonies—a prediction fulfilled all but to the letter? These are his memorable words: "When Canada comes to be conquered, and when the Canadians and these colonists form one people, do you imagine that they will remain any longer in subjection from the moment England appears to touch their interest?....I am sure of what I write, and would allow no more than ten years for its accomplishment after Canada falls."

Biography of Chevalier de Lévis

BETWEEN the Marquis de Montcalm and the Chevalier de Lévis there seems to have been established, during their years in Canada, the bond of brotherhood, from the day on which the former wrote to his mother on his departure from France to America: "I like the Chevalier de Lévis and I think he likes me," just as later he wrote: "I cannot speak too well of him. Without being a man of brilliant parts, he has good experience, good sense, and a quick eye; and, though I had served with him before, I never should have thought he possessed such promptitude and efficiency. He has turned his campaigns to good account."

The Chevalier de Lévis was born in 1720, in Languedoc, having for his birth-place the chateau or country-seat in which the Duc de Ventadour of Champlain's time was also born. He had won renown in Bohemia, in Germany, and in Italy, in the years before he was commissioned to join the Marquis de Montcalm in America. As may be remembered, he had charge of the right wing of Montcalm's army at the battle of Carillon, or Ticonderoga, where he added to his laurels for soldierly bravery and skill. While the siege of Quebec was yet going on, he was sent to Montreal at the instance of Governor. Vaudreuil; and when, after the seizure of the city by General Townshend, he returned to retake the place in 1760, and won the battle of Sainte-Foye, his fame as a soldier became, in the opinion of many of his compatriots, even greater than Montcalm's own, if only for a time.

Nor was he without the very highest opinion of his general. "I do not know if the Marquis de Montcalm is pleased with me," he once wrote home, "but I am sure that I am very much so with him, and shall always be charmed to serve under his orders. It is not for me, Monseigneur, to speak to you of his merit and his talents. You know him better than anyone else; but I may have the honour of assuring you that he has pleased everybody in this colony, and manages affairs with the Indians extremely well." And though De Lévis must have known that all was not well with the relationship between Governor Vaudreuil and his general, the panegyric was no less sincere, giving us, as it does, a glimpse at one of the leading features in the character of Montcalm's second in command, which led him to be on good terms with both. "One should be on good terms with everybody," was one of his maxims, and we all know how it led to his own popularity in social circles as well as military.

It must not be thought, however, that De Lévis was a man of wavering purpose, when the occasion demanded instant action. For example, when Vaudreuil sent him word from Quebec that the French had been driven from the battlefield, he set out post haste to check the rout; demanding that the Governor should order the army back to the lines at Beauport. "The great number of fugitives that I began to meet at Three Rivers prepared me," as he said afterwards in his report, "for the disorder in which I found the army. I

never in my life knew the like of it. They left everything behind in the camp at Beauport; tents, baggage
and kettles....I therefore engaged M. de Vaudreuil
to march the army back to the relief of the place. I
represented to him that this was the only way to prevent the complete defection of the Canadians and the
Indians; that our knowledge of the country would
enable us to approach very near the enemy, whom we
knew to be intrenching themselves on the heights of
Quebec, and constructing batteries to breach the walls;
that if we found their army ill posted, we would attack them, or, at any rate, could prolong the siege by
throwing men and supplies into the town; and that,
if we could not save it, we could evacuate and burn
it, so that the enemy could not possibly winter there."

Too late as it was, the plan was readily accepted
by Vaudreuil and those of his counsels. De Lévis
meant what he had said to the Governor; and we have
another token of his true character, in a note which
he hurriedly wrote to Bourlamaque, as he was on the
point of proceeding to rally the retreating army, and
turn the stragglers back to Quebec. "We have had a
very great loss, for we have lost M. de Montcalm. I
regret him as my general and my friend. I have
found our army here. It is now on the march back
to retrieve our fortunes. I can trust you to hold your
position. As I have not M. de Montcalm's talents,
I look to you to second me and advise me. Put a
good face on it. Hide this business as long as you
can. I am mounting my horse this moment. Write
me all the news."

The sequel to all this energy of mind and body on
the part of De Lévis is well known. He conducted

the army as far as St. Augustin, and there he heard that Ramézay had given the town up to Townshend and Saunders.

. Seven months afterwards he tried to make good his efforts to save Quebec to the French. When he was forced to retreat from his entrenchments on the Plains of Abraham, on the arrival of Admiral Colville's ships to relieve Murray, whom he had hemmed in within the walls, he took up his headquarters at Montreal, which he is said to have been ready to defend to the bitter end, but for the wavering of Vaudreuil, who, ostensibly working hand and glove with him, was only brave in his despatches. And we know how he stood out bravely for the best terms possible, when Vaudreuil in his vacillation at length submitted. After Canada had been ceded to Great Britain, De Lévis went back to his native country, taking part in the closing scenes of the Seven Years' War, and being with the Prince of Condé when he defeated Prince Ferdinand in the battle of Johannisbourg. Before his death in 1787, he was created a Marshal of France, and was raised to the peerage of that country under the title of Duc de Lévis.

Between him and Montcalm, as one may surmise, there never was to be seen the faintest trace of professional pique, however Vaudreuil did his best, on more than one occasion, to provoke a rivalry between them. When the Chevalier obeyed Vaudreuil's orders to return to Montreal, while the enemy was still threatening the Beauport lines, Montcalm must have felt as if he had lost his best support. There is a memoir on record to the effect that Vaudreuil prevented De Lévis from taking more than fifteen hundred men with

him from Montreal when he was called upon to join
Montcalm at Quebec; and the suspicion has not been
wholly dispelled that the same intermeddler in military affairs had something to do with De Lévis' premature
withdrawal from the immediate support of his general
at Beauport.   Be this as it may, there has never been
traced the slightest stain upon Chevalier De Lévis'
intrepidity, loyalty and skill, as a soldier worthy to
succeed the brave Montcalm; although, at the same
time, it is futile and invidious for any one to keep con-
jecturing, as Vaudreuil did after the death of Montcalm, how the course of events might have been turned,
had he been serving under Montcalm's immediate
command.

De Lévis was with Montcalm at Carillon.   And at
the moment of the exultancy over the French victory,
he was at one with Montcalm, however friendly he
was with Vaudreuil, that without reinforcements from
France and further military supplies, there was no
likelihood of a final saving of the situation in New
France, against Great Britain and its war resources.
Montcalm at this time was so impressed with the mal-
administration of affairs in Canada, that he asked for
his recall.   As he well perceived, with De Lévis and
Bougainville and others of his officers, his mixed forces
had to contend with an enemy "resolute, persevering,
and superior in numbers and resources of all kinds."
And the views of Montcalm and De Lévis on the actual
state of affairs were finally emphasized, when Bougainville went to France to convince the home government
that there was nothing but disaster for the French
prestige in Canada, if the administration of public
affairs was to remain as it was.

Indeed, with all the facts of the situation now un-
hidden, it is quite safe to say that Canada was lost to
France from no lack of skill or courage on the part of
Montcalm and his three most prominent military
coadjutors, De Lévis, Bougainville and Bourlamaque.
They all proved their competency to manage a campaign. There was the strength of a courageous co-
operation in their personal friendship and faith in one
another. And this strength was no doubt the central
thought in Montcalm's mind, when in the extremity
of death he said: "If I could survive this wound, I
would engage to beat three times the number of such
forces as I commanded this morning, with a third of
such troops as those which were opposed to me." At
least he could not fail to regret that not one of his three
personal friends whom he had brought out with him
from France, had been by his side on the battlefield
that had decided his fate.

And how different is all this to the petty dealing
on the part of Vaudreuil, when he recommended the
Chevalier de Lévis as the dead commander's successor!
"The Marquis de Montcalm could not be more worthily
replaced than by the Chevalier de Lévis," is what he
said to his council out on the horn-work of Ringfield.
"It is even now to be desired that he had commanded
the army from the very commencement of the campaign; and I am convinced that if he had been near
Montcalm on September the 13th, the course of events
would have been very different to what it has been."

De Lévis was not a man to be deceived by such
a compliment. Though he had never been on ill terms
with Vaudreuil, as he was seldom with any of his associates, he was no more submissive to a lame authority

than Montcalm had been. He was angry when he heard that Ramézay had given up the city, suggested as it had been by Vaudreuil, just as he refused to hide his indignation when Vaudreuil in his own person surrendered the whole of Canada at the demand of General Amherst. In the words of his brave predecessor in the generalship: "Chevalier de Lévis was a highly talented man, with a lofty military spirit and decision of character, indefatigable, and conversant with military routine, and every step in his career as a soldier has happily proven it to posterity, with no hiding away of evidence to enhance the record."

The outcome of the victory he gained over his adversary at Sainte-Foye was his investment of the city from the Plains of Abraham.   His trenches extended all the way from Wolfe's Cove to the Belvedere Brook. The French ships brought him supplies by way of the Cove. Meantime Murray was doing his best to improve his means of defence; and, for over a fortnight, there was kept up a steady exchange of cannonading, culminating in more strenuous and disastrous firing when De Lévis had approached to within seven hundred yards or so of the walls. At length the arrival of the English frigates turned the scales against the persistency of the Chevalier. They came in one after the other; and, when two of them had seized the French transports up at the Cove, and began to enfilade the French trenches with their shells, there was nothing for discretion but to raise the siege. This was done on the night of the 12th of May; and so skilfully did De Lévis contrive his retreat along the highways leading to Cap Rouge and further, that no opportunity was given to the English to exploit a successful pursuit. Many of the French guns were left in their redoubts, as well as supplies in the store-tents. By the time he had reached Cap Rouge, the volunteers of the army began to disappear. And when the indefatigable commander had reached Three Rivers, desertion from the ranks had become epidemic. On his entry into Montreal, all that was left of the "ten thousand" that had followed him to Quebec, were the regulars and the militia of Montreal, the regulars themselves having been reduced in numbers on account of the garrisons left at Cap Rouge, Three Rivers and Sorel.

When Montreal capitulated, De Lévis stood true to his patriotic spirit. He protested, in no diplomatic smoothness of speech, against many of the terms of the capitulation while they were being discussed; and even when his indignation had been set at naught by Vaudreuil, and Amherst had accomplished his purpose without the shedding of blood, he is said to have declared to his immediate associates that he was prepared to retreat with all who would accompany him to Helen's Island and there hold out to the last extremity, rather than give his assent to some of the proposals Vaudreuil was willing to accept. His was the indignation of a misguided patriot, no doubt. At least his wrathful protests were unheeded. Nor was there any eagerness to stand by him in his proposal to take up a last stand on Helen's Island. And so when it was all over—Quebec, Montreal, and the whole country delivered up to a change of masters—De Lévis embarked for France.

On his return, there was a trying time awaiting many of those with whom he had had intercourse during his three years' stay in Canada. Several of these, including Bigot and his boodle-minded *entourage*, had the way of the transgressor to walk on their arrival, with a dungeon in the Bastile, and after-exile at the end of it for them. But to the intrepid Chevalier there was nothing but honour awaiting him, with promotion in the army open for his acceptance. There were brave men—thousands of them—among the soldiers who defended Quebec in its darkest days; and it is needless to say that one of the very bravest of these was the Chevalier de Lévis, afterwards the Duc de Lévis, of the Chateau d'Anjac en Languedoc, whose statue in bronze graces, with those of others whom Canada delights to honour, the facade of the Parliament Building of Quebec.

The artist who painted the picture we have of the Chevalier de Lévis has represented him as being a person of full round face, rather low of forehead, and with eyes in which gentleness vies with eagerness of purpose. In the representation there is less of the intrepid soldier we all love to read about, and more of the ordinary bidding for favour; and when we look at it for the first time, we think more of the gay side of his disposition than of his resoluteness in battle.

Biography of Colonel Bougainville

ONE cannot escape the polemic surmise as to what would have been the issue on the 13th of September, 1759, had Chevalier de Lévis and Colonel Bougainville been on the field to support General Montcalm, in his respective wings. Louis Antoine Bougainville had made a name for himself in public life before he left France to take part in the colonial war of America. He had been born, the son of a notary, in Paris, in 1729. His university career had been a brilliant one, bringing him distinction in his mathematical studies. On leaving college, he had first selected the legal profession for a vocation, being admitted a counsellor-at-law, and becoming an advocate in the Parliament of Paris. In his twenty-third year, he published an important work of two volumes on the *Integral Calculus*. The times, however, were rife with the excitements of the military life, and young Bougainville, laying aside his design of being a lawyer, entered the French army as an adjutant in the provincial battalion of Picardy. For a time he was engaged as one of General Chevert's aides-de-camp, until he was taken from his post to proceed to London, as a Secretary of the French Embassy there. While in England his erudition was honoured by his being elected a member of the Royal Society.

199

Before the Marquis de Montcalm was appointed to take command in America, he had heard not a little of Bougainville as a young soldier and a savant of promise; and it was a pleasant surprise to both of them when the latter was appointed one of the general's aides-de-camp to accompany him to Canada. And safely it may be said, that no more loyal friend or trustworthy adviser could Montcalm have found than the young counsellor-at-law, who, while even yet making his mark as a mathematician, was seized with the passion of winning glory beyond the precincts of Parliament, or the cloisters of a university. Bougainville set sail for the St. Lawrence, in the vessel which had his superior officer on board, in the spring of 1756. "What a nation is ours!" exclaimed the young subaltern, as he looked upon the troops embarking with all the gayety imaginable. "Happy is he who commands it, and commands it worthily!"

As we know, there were strange goings on in New France at this time—a mixed morality in the affairs of state, an extravagance of living among the rich, a grovelling distress among the poor. And, about one of the first things that struck Bougainville on his arrival at Quebec, was the way in which the exiled Acadians were being treated by the French-Canadians. It was but a foreshadowing of the treatment his own general was to encounter from the petty jealousy of Vaudreuil and the Bigot "Canadian Party."

"These poor people," he tells us in his journal, "are dying by wholesale. Their past and present misery, joined to the rapacity of the Canadians, who seek only to squeeze out of them all the money they can get from them, and then refuse them the help so dearly bought, is the main cause of this mortality. For example, a townsman of Quebec was in debt to one of the partners of the Great Company (Bigot's combine), and had no means of paying his debt. The said company gave him a large number of Acadians to board and lodge, and he starved them with hunger and cold, got out of them what money they had, and paid the extortioners. What a country! What a treatment of those of their own origin!''

The seat of war was far from Quebec, westward to the great lakes and southward to the headwaters of Lake Champlain. And Bougainville's first experiences in the colonial war were had with Montcalm at the taking of Oswego—the prelude to the series of successes against the English in the neighbourhood of Lake George. Bougainville was the officer who presented to the Oswegoans the terms of capitulation, which were at once accepted, to be followed by scenes of plunder, debauch, and scalping on the part of Montcalm's Indian allies, that neither he nor Bougainville could restrain, until the rage of the savages, joined in by many of the Canadians, was more than half spent. It was a new kind of warfare for French regulars to witness, and fairly sickened the generous-minded Bougainville when he first came to see it.

But he was to learn more of such warfare when he went out from Ticonderoga with Marin, the Canadian bush-fighter, on an expedition under the nominal command of Captain Perière. ''Of all caprice,'' says he in his journal, ''Indian caprice is the most capricious.'' And when the raid was over, with little or nothing accomplished, save a repetition of the savage exhilarations witnessed a short time previously at

Oswego, Montcalm's aide-de-camp had his ideas of war put to the blush, as he saw with disgust the abominations practised by the Indians while on the war-path with the Canadians. "The very recital of the cruelties they committed on the battlefield is horrible," he writes. "The ferocity and insolence of these black-souled barbarians, even towards us, their friends, makes one shudder. It is an abominable kind of war. The air one breathes is contagion of insensibility and hardness."

And yet such allies had to be secured in presence of Montcalm's need for a paid soldiery, with Bigot squandering the fiscal resources of the colony under Vaudreuil's eye; and, what is more, Colonel Bougain-ville, under orders, had to treat with these savages for their amity and aid. "I sang their war-song," he again tells us, after coming from one of their war-councils. "I sang it in the name of M. de Montcalm, and was applauded. It was nothing but these words, 'Let us trample the English under our feet,' chanted over and over again, in cadence with their movements." And if one should wish to make a study of the degra-dation of these red allies, or the greater degradation to a white race in employing such in their wars, he will find it all in Bougainville's journal.

"What a scourge!" he exclaims in one passage, after writing of their insolence and tyranny in their behaviour towards their own white friends on their way against a common enemy—of their drunkenness, their cruelty and cannibalism. "What a scourge! Humanity groans at being forced to use such mon-sters. What can be done against an invisible enemy of their sort, who strike and then vanish? It is the destroying angel."

How much more was it in keeping with the chivalry of Bougainville's character to be entrusted with the transfer of important military messages than to be sent to court favour with the redman! He was ever in the heart of affairs while he was with Montcalm endeavouring to strengthen the position of the French at Ticonderoga. When Fort William Henry, at the extreme end of Lake George, was in straits from the soldiery of Montcalm, and a letter was sent from Fort Edward, a few miles inland from the lake, to the effect that Colonel Webb, stationed at the latter fort, could not send assistance to Colonel Munro, in charge of the former, the letter fell into the hands of Montcalm. After keeping it for some days, the French general entrusted it to his aide-de-camp, to have it conveyed to Colonel Munro's own hands. Bougainville undertook the duty in person, and, preceded by a drummer and a soldier with a flag in his hand, he allowed himself to be blindfolded at the foot of the glacis of Fort William Henry, and thereafter to be conducted into the presence of the English colonel. The sequel is referred to in Bougainville's own words:

"Colonel Munro returned many thanks for the courtesy of our nation, and protested his joy at having to do with so generous an enemy. This was his answer to the Marquis de Montcalm. Then they led me back, with eyes once more blindfolded; and our batteries began to fire again as soon as we thought that the English grenadiers who escorted me had had time to re-enter the fort. I hope General Webb's letter may induce the English to surrender all the sooner."

After Fort William Henry had fallen, Bougainville was again the messenger employed by Montcalm to carry the news to Governor Vaudreuil at Montreal. And thus the sensitive messenger escaped being an eye-witness of the tribal allies of the French, in their dreadful massacre of the British soldiery that followed the taking of the place.

By this time, moreover, his eyes were opened to the network of intrigue that was intended to imperil the authority of his general, as well as to the pilfering that was weakening the monetary affairs of the colony. And Bougainville has made note of much of both in his journal, not without a reading of his own indignation at it, all between the lines. "Why is it," he asks, "that of all which the king sends to the Indians, two-thirds of it is stolen, and the rest sold to them instead of being given?" And when he enumerates the few who are guiltless of peculation in the rush for ill-gotten wealth, he facetiously hints that they are not "enough to save Sodom."

Nor did he hide from himself the deficiencies in the character of the Governor. In fact, he goes so far as to say that Vaudreuil had it in mind on one occasion to arrange for a reverse to his own people, in order that his pique against Montcalm might be gratified by bringing discredit on his command. And, after the victorious defence of Ticonderoga, in which Bougainville was wounded, he was to find out how far Vaudreuil's duplicity could go, even in his own case, when he was chosen to sail for France to report direct to the Colonial Office the condition of affairs in New France, which few in Canada did not know had become deplorable.

After the affair at Ticonderoga, Montcalm had asked for his own recall. On second thoughts, however, he sent home an after-despatch saying that since ruin stared the colony in the face, he would remain at his post to do what he could to retard its fall. To gain assistance, however, he urged that some one should be sent to France to lay bare the state of affairs in the colony, and Vaudreuil did not dare refuse Montcalm's request to allow Bougainville to go to France as the right man to send. But before the general's aide-de-camp set sail, the latter wrote a letter of introduction, which he placed for delivery in Bougainville's own hands, and another to reach the Colonial Minister by another channel. In the first letter he recommended the bearer as one better qualified than anyone else to give reliable information concerning the state of the colony. "I have given M. Bougainville my instructions, and you can trust entirely in what he tells you." At the end of the second letter, however, the wily Governor, daring the duplicity of the act alike towards Bougainville and the Colonial Minister says: "In order to condescend to the wishes of M. de Montcalm, and leave no means untried to keep in harmony with him, I have given letters to MM. Doreil and Bougainville; but I have the honour to inform you that they do not understand the colony and to warn you that they are the creatures of M. de Montcalm."

The two ambassadors arrived safely. M. Berryer was the Colonial Minister to whom M. de Vaudreuil had written his double-faced recommendations. And M. Berryer, being on close, friendly terms with Vaudreuil, seemed to be only too glad to turn the cold shoulder on Montcalm's earnest request for help. But Bougainville, possessed of some experience as an ambassador, did not rest until he had reached the ear of

Madame Pompadour; and, though that *dame du roi*
could make no promise of money help—for the revenues of France were at almost as low a tide at the
time as were those of New France—she was not ˙slow
to secure favours of another kind to bestow upon the
victors of Carillon, a victory which the French had
made a good deal of, considering their frequent re-
verses on the battlefields of Europe. She induced the
king to make Montcalm a lieutenant-general, Lévis
a major-general, Bourlamaque a brigadier, Bougainville a colonel and Chevalier de, St. Louis; while Vaudreuil was awarded the grand cross of St. Louis.

But Bougainville, after seeing all the ministers and
the king himself, made his memorials stronger and
stronger, and at last succeeded in obtaining a promise
of four hundred recruits for the regulars in Canada,
sixty engineers and artillerymen, and supplies sufficient for another winter's campaign. Nor did he leave
France until he had given a further token of his loyalty
to his general's personal affairs, by arranging the terms
of marriage between Montcalm's son and a rich heiress,
as well as attending to the marriage contract of his
general's daughter, all of which he was well qualified as
a lawyer to do.

When Bougainville went back to Canada, he carried
with him such advice from the authorities at Paris
as a poverty-stricken grandee might give to a poor
relation. "However small may be the space you are
able to hold, it is indispensable to keep a footing in
North America; for if we once lose the country entirely,
its recovery will be impossible. The king counts on
your zeal, courage, and persistency to accomplish
this object, and relies on you to spare no pains and

no exertions. Impart this resolution to your chief officers, and join with them to inspire your soldiers with it." This came from the Maréchal de Belleisle, who excuses the sending of a larger reinforcement than Bougainville had secured, by saying that the English would be sure to overtake it on the seas, or provide a much larger one to oppose it. "I have answered for you to the king; I am confident that you will not disappoint me, and that for the glory of the nation, the good of the state, and your own preservation, you will go to the utmost extremity rather than submit to conditions as shameful as those imposed at Louisbourg, the memory of which you will wipe out."

And we know what Montcalm's answer was to such an appeal, both by word and deed: "We will save this unhappy colony, or perish," he said, and it was his faithful messenger Bougainville who heard him say it, as he himself made up his mind to stand by him, in the resolution, even if he knew for certain before he left France that the English were preparing a large armament to attack Quebec.

The news that he brought about this armament necessarily alarmed the whole town; and in a day or two the intelligence seemed to be ratified sooner than was expected; for a fleet of eighteen vessels was seen one day sailing up the harbour from the turn in the south channel near the Island of Orleans. The consternation of the populace, however, was soon allayed, when it came to be known that they were the supply vessels which Bougainville and his associate ambassador had been able to have promise of before leaving France. For a week or so the name of Bougainville was in everyone's mouth on the streets of Quebec;

for the moment he was looked upon as the saviour of the town.

Nor had any one more faith than Colonel Bougainville in the strength of Quebec to withstand the largest force England was likely to send up the St. Lawrence. "By the help of entrenchments, easily and quickly made, I think the city should be safe," was what he kept saying to his associates, when the order went out to have a concentration of all the available fighting men in the vicinity made along the Beauport shore, and in the town itself. Before the enemy hove in sight, moreover, he was selected by Montcalm, who knew his man, to assume one of the most difficult tasks of the campaign. He was to take charge of the encampment at Cap Rouge, from which outpost he was to keep a watch on the steep embankments of the main river, all the way from Pointe-aux-Trembles to Sillery. And the way he fulfilled his task is on record. He repulsed General Murray at Pointe-aux-Trembles, and even as far up as Deschambault caused the English to withdraw, though not without loss of supplies to the French; while below Cap Rouge he checked the invaders more than once, if only for a time. And it is not unfair to say that had the outpost at the *Anse du Foulon* been under his immediate command, the British army would have had more of a task than they even had in climbing to the levels of the plateau behind the town.

The story of Bougainville's life at this time is the story of the siege. He has been blamed for not following Holmes's ships on their last trip down the river with the tide. But Holmes's vessels had sailed down with the tide more than once before, as if only to delude the watchers at Cap Rouge. The movement was in the general plan of the attack, but even Wolfe's own soldiers did not know what it all portended. He has also been blamed for not arriving at the scene of the battle earlier. But he did leave Cap Rouge a little after eight in the morning, and Cap Rouge is a good nine miles from Quebec. The battle commenced at ten in the morning, and in ten minutes' time or thereabout, Montcalm's army was in full flight. Bougainville was not behind time to face Townshend, after the main rout had taken place; but we know what Townshend was obliged to plead in his own defence, for refusing to face the three thousand men Bougainville brought with him from Cap Rouge. Wolfe's successor in the field refused to give battle to Bougainville, and what could the latter do under the circumstances but seek a retreat in the Sillery woods?

"Ah, what a cruel day!" was all the brave soldier could say in his retreat. "How fatal to all that was dearest to us! My heart is torn in its most tender parts. We shall be fortunate if the approach of winter saves the country from total ruin."

Soon after, he was to be found in his old quarters at Cap Rouge, awaiting events. When the city was surrendered by Ramézay, he joined De Lévis on his way back to Montreal, after the latter had made a hastened visit to Quebec to pick up the fragments of the French army. The next we hear of him is at Isle-aux-Noix, on the Richelieu, where he had been sent to bar the approach of the English by way of Lake Champlain. Thence he found his way to Montreal just as Vaudreuil was calling a council meeting to arrange, with or without the approbation of De Lévis and his brother officers, the terms of the capitulation of the whole country to Great Britain. Bougainville was again the messenger between the negotiating parties. His first reception by Amherst was unfavourable. He returned a second time with terms more agreeable—the terms that were finally accepted. When the country changed hands, there was, as has been said, a general deportation of the leading men of the colony to France, and among them was Colonel Louis Antoine Bougainville, who was yet young enough to make a name for himself as navigator in the service of his country.

After serving for a year or so as aide-de-camp to General de Choiseul-Stainville, and after being given charge of a small fleet sailing from St. Malo, to make good the claim of the Spaniards to the Malouine Islands, he went on a voyage of discovery in the South Seas, visiting the Society Islands, the New Hebrides, New Guinea, and other insular groups on his way round the world. In his forty-fourth year he published a full account of his travels in a volume which is still worth reading. As he had been made a colonel for his services in the French army, so was he made a commodore for his services in the French navy. He lived to the ripe old age of eighty-two, full of honours, a Senator of France and a Member of the Institute, with a place at the Bureau des Longitudes.

Colonel Bougainville's face, as seen in the portrait we have of him, is one to win, not from any soldierly sturdiness of character in its lines, as from the gentle forbearance and introspection in the traits around his eyes and kindly mouth. He has been made to look older than the man whom we read of in history as the faithful friend and intrepid soldier; but there is everything in the expression of his features to tell us how well fitted.he was to treat with kings and courtiers on their own ground.

Biography of
Brigadier de Bourlamaque

Of the three officers who accompanied the Marquis de Montcalm to Canada, neither the Chevalier de Lévis, his second in command, nor Colonel Bougainville, next in military rank, seemed to have any more of his confidence than M. de Bourlamaque, his third aide-de-camp. And of this third aide-de-camp there is but little known, save the record of his bravery and astute address as a soldier in the colonial war which ended in the cession of Canada to Great Britain. He came to Canada with Montcalm, and returned to France with the deportation of the leading Frenchmen of the colony at the time when General Murray became its first British governor. He died while holding the post of Governor of Guadaloupe, and is referred to, by the most of our historians, as the Chevalier de Bourlamaque; but of the early scenes of his boyhood or studenthood we virtually know nothing.

He was not at Quebec at the time of its siege by Wolfe. He had served under Montcalm at Ticonderoga, and when the concentration of the forces in the colony took place at Quebec, he was at the Isle-aux-Noix, guarding the Richelieu against the approach of New England help from the region round Lake

213

Champlain and of General Amherst, on his way to Montreal from Albany. How he came to be stationed at Isle-aux-Noix is a matter of history.

During Montcalm's defence of Ticonderoga, Bourlamaque was in charge of the battalions of Béarn and Royal Rousillon, with his eagle's eye directed to the coverts around Fort William Henry and the head waters of Lake George. In the struggle with the British around the ramparts of Ticonderoga, he was dangerously wounded, and it was while he was reaching the stage of convalescence, that the news came from Quebec that Montcalm was required there. Montcalm had spoken in the highest terms of his wounded comrade: "Alone with Lévis and Bourlamaque and the troop of the line, thirty-one hundred fighting men in all, I have beaten an army of twenty-five thousand." And it was no wonder that the king was induced to bestow the honour of a brigadiership on Bourlamaque, while distributing honours among the victors.

When Montcalm left Ticonderoga for Quebec, M. de Bourlamaque was left in charge of that fort. The fourfold plan of the Duke of Cumberland had by this time driven the Acadians from Nova Scotia, Niagara had succumbed, Amherst was at Albany waiting to make connection with the New Englanders in his projected descent on Montreal by way of Lake Champlain and the valley of the Richelieu, while Quebec was on the point of being confronted with an army direct from England. But for the buoyancy of hope in the French defenders, it looked as if the French were to be driven from North America, unless they submitted to a change of masters.

Bourlamaque knew only too well that the fort left in his charge could not withstand a second attack from such a general as Amherst, in command of a united force from the west and south. And when he learned definitely that Amherst was on the way with an overwhelming force, he laid mines under the ramparts and the inner buildings of the place, and withdrew with the bulk of his garrison to Crown Point, a few miles distant further down the narrows, as if there to await the arrival of the English, and see what would happen when they found Ticonderoga deserted. What did happen does not raise Bourlamaque in our estimation. It was hardly in the way of fair fighting. For, when the English advance-guard sought entrance to the deserted fort, they were greeted by an explosion as if from an earthquake that laid the place in ruins. When the English had taken possession of the ruins, making their encampment all around them, Bourlamaque at once retreated from Crown Point in his boats, down the lake and the river, to Isle-aux-Noix. Meantime Amherst, unable to secure the necessary transportation craft, had to make up his mind to winter at Ticonderoga and Crown Point, making the most of his ingenuity in building boats for his service in spring.

While at Isle-aux-Noix, Bourlamaque became more and more sanguine of success. His scouts had no doubt informed him of the difficulties which beset Amherst in the matter of means for the transportation of his troops. "I await the coming of the enemy with impatience," he says in a letter to headquarters, "though I doubt if he will venture to attack a fort where we are intrenched to the teeth, and armed with a hundred pieces of cannon." And truly the post on Isle-aux-Noix was not only well fortified, but possessed of a garrison of three thousand five hundred men. Besides, it was easy of access to Montreal, where De Lévis had taken up his quarters with fifteen hundred men. Indeed, Bourlamaque continued confident that the islet on which he had made his encampment was all but impregnable. His hopes were high over the affairs of the colony also. He had had letters from Quebec written by Vaudreuil, Montcalm and others, in which he had been told of the repulse at Montmorency, Vaudreuil informing him with the utmost confidence that he was in daily expectation of seeing Wolfe and his battalions sailing for England. "Everything proves,' he wrote, "that the grand design of the English has failed."

And Montcalm also wrote sanguinely to him: "I wish you were here, for I cannot be everywhere, though I multiply myself, and have not taken off my clothes since the twenty-third of June. I am overwhelmed with work, and should often lose temper, like you, if I did not remember that I am paid by Europe for not losing it. Nothing new since my last. I give the enemy another month, or something less, to stay here."

In the affair of 1760—the Battle of Sainte-Foye—Brigadier Bourlamaque was with De Lévis, at Quebec. He and Bougainville had changed places, the latter being stationed at Isle-aux-Noix, as yet unmolested by Amherst. In the thick of the fight around Dumont's Mill on the Ste. Foye Road, Bourlamaque had his horse killed under him. But there was no stay to his courage. Again and again he rallied his division to the charge, following the English in retreat along the highway towards the city's walls. And not until De Lévis left for Montreal, after the arrival of Colville's fleet, did he forsake his command, assisting the general in his somewhat inglorious retreat, and doing his best to prevent the regulars from being seized with the spirit of desertion exhibited by the volunteers. When the capitulation took place of the whole country, there was then nothing for him to do but to carry home his clean record as a best recommendation for promotion in the army of France.

Brigadier Bourlamaque certainly enjoyed the confidence of M. de Montcalm, one might almost say to the point of indiscretion. The freedom of the latter's letters to his aide-de-camp give not a little light-and-shade, however, to our knowledge of Quebec society in these early days, with Madame Péan's house on St. Louis Street as a centre of gossip and worse, with the ladies of Parloir Street, who could have had nothing to do with the Convent near by, taking their share in the garrison frolics, and the house of Madame Pennissault opening its hospitable doors to such as the jilted husband of Angelique de Meloise at one time and the Chevalier de Lévis at another.

"I burn your letters, monsieur," Montcalm once wrote to him, "and I beg you to do the same with mine, after making note of anything you want to keep." But Chevalier de Bourlamaque, thinking, no doubt, that everything Montcalm wrote was worth keeping, put every letter he received from him on file, and to-day they are to be found bound in a volume in the safe-keeping of our archives, or reproduced in print.

During the winter of 1758-59, Bourlamaque, with Bougainville and De Lévis, were fully aware of the true character of Vaudreuil and his game at cross-purposes with the general. And how intimate he must have been in the counsels of Montcalm is put in evidence by such a communication as this from Montcalm: "God or devil, we must do something and risk a fight. If we succeed, we can all three ask for promotion. Burn this letter." And again: "Come as soon as you can, and I will tell a certain fair lady how eager you are."

The story of the four comrades would form the ground-work for a good romance under some such a title as "The Four Chevaliers in Canada," the one character helping us to read the other aright. And there is no lack of spice for such a narrative, since the gallantries of Chevalier de Lévis culminated in his taking Madame Pennissault back to France with him. In the city, or even in camp, there were suppers and social gayeties. For instance, when the French soldiers were on their way to the seat of war, Montcalm went over to La Prairie to see them off, and this is how he speaks of the festivities which followed, in a letter to his confidant, Bourlamaque: "I reviewed the soldiers and gave the officers a dinner, which, if anybody else had given it, I should have said was a grand affair. There were two tables, for thirty-six persons in all. On Wednesday there was an Assembly at Madame Varin's; on Friday the Chevalier de Lévis gave a ball. He invited sixty-five ladies, and got only thirty, with a great crowd of men. Rooms well lighted, excellent order, excellent service, plenty of refreshments of every sort all through the night; and the company stayed till seven in the morning. As for me, I went to bed early. I had had that day eight ladies at a supper, given to I don't know whom, but I incline to think it will be La Roche Beaucour. The gallant Chevalier is to give us still another ball."

And there are other letters of the same kind dealing with the festivities of the time, and among them one dealing with the Lenten season and its duties: "I shall throw myself into the devotions religiously. It will be easier for me to detach myself from the world and turn heavenward here than at Quebec." And again he tells how, during the same solemn season, Bougainville spent a devout hour or so with the Sulpicians, and how he himself supped with them in their refectory in the evening.

The three comrades set sail for France in the fleet that bore the French regulars back to Europe, at least all of them who resisted the temptation of deserting. They had an unhappy voyage, storm succeeding storm, as if the elements were conspiring to provide for them a watery grave. The welcome of the three was not overwhelmed in the gloom of the national disaster which had culminated in the death of Montcalm and the loss of Canada. In time, they were all promoted in the military service of their country.

Miscellaneous Notes

The Names of the Battlefield. The name given to the battlefield arose from the fact that a part of the plateau, beyond the farms of Hébert and Couillard, was originally occupied for grazing purposes by a settler of the name of Abraham Martin, said to have been a pilot of Scottish descent. The name remains in Côté d'Abraham, the connecting sloping thoroughfare between the suburbs of St. John and St. Roch. The land owned by Maitre Abraham, as he was called by his neighbours, consisted of thirty-two acres to the west of what afterwards became the wall line of the city, and the site of the suburbs of St. Louis and St. John; and the name seems in early times to have been extended, by use and wont, to the sloping ground and plateau beyond, until finally it came to be applied to the whole tract as far as the *Anse du Foulon* and Dumont's Mill on the Ste. Foye Road, near where the *Monument aux Braves* now stands. The Ursulines eventually came into possession of part of these lands, and naturally enough, when they gave to the Imperial authorities in 1802 a ninety-nine years' lease of their property for reviewing purposes, the name clung to that part, as has been elsewhere explained, in connection with military reviews and other outdoor exercises. Elsewhere also a suggestion has been made as to the origin of the name Sainte-Foye. When the river Montmorency was first thus called is not known, but there is hardly any doubt that it was given in honour of the Duc de Montmorenci, the viceroy of New France in Champlain's day; although it must be remembered that Bishop Laval was a Montmorency, and that may have had something to do with the perpetuation of the name. There is no subject more interesting about Quebec than a study of the origin of the place-names within its environs, from the names of its streets to the names of the villages, streams and heights of land in its vicinity.

The Respective Numbers of the Armies. This is a vexed question with the historians, and is always being revised. The British army under Wolfe, taking part in the battle of 1759, comprised 4,829 rank and file, and 250 officers and staff. The total number of men in Wolfe's three brigades, which disembarked from the fleet on the Island of Orleans on the 27th of June, was 8,600. The numbers of the French army stationed along the lines of the Beauport defence from the city to Montmorency are variously computed at from 12,000 to 16,000, the fluctuation, whatever it was, being a corroboration of the number of desertions that took place before the 13th of September. It is safe to say that there were at least 7,500 of these present on the plains the morning of the battle. As Miles says: "The French accounts, except perhaps that of Bigot, leave us to infer that their forces were less numerous than the British." Then again, in the battle of Sainte-Foye, Garneau claims that there were 7,714 British soldiers in the field, though where they came from no one can tell, seeing General Murray declares that he had only 4,817 men who were not on the sick list in the city. If De Lévis' army grew to be 10,000 strong by the time he reached Quebec from Montreal, and Murray states what is true in his despatch over the affair that of the 3,000 men he had in the field with him he lost a third, we get as near to the comparative strength of the forces engaged as it is possible. Corroborative of Murray's statement in his despatch, the army roll shows that there were only 3,341 fit for duty four days before the battle. Of the killed and wounded in the repulse at Montmorency, there were 400 British and not more than 50 French; in the Battle of the Plains, there were 755 British killed and wounded, and 1,600 French; in the battle of Sainte-Foye there were 1,000 British killed and wounded and 2,500 French. The inequality between the armies was not so much in numbers as in training and experience, Montcalm having under him, beyond his Imperial brigades, a mixed force of colonial militia, Indian irregulars, and Canadian volunteers, who could hardly be expected to withstand an attack from the veterans of Louisbourg and the European battlefields except from behind such ramparts as those at Carillon and Montmorency.

The Natural Features of the Plains. The open spaces, as seen from the Buttes-à-Neveu in these days, were covered for the most part with stunted shrubs and burr-bushes. These open spaces were interrupted by three noteworthy coppices of varied tree-growth—first, the one immediately outside the city walls not far from the site of the present Parliament Buildings; second, the Ste. Genevieve woods traversed by the Ste. Foye Road, near what is now called Sauvageau Hill; and the third, on what is now De Salaberry Street, and covering the present site of the grounds of the St. Bridget Asylum. Here and there, were several windmills, notably Dumont's Mill, and the one which occupied the site of the present Martello Tower, near the Grande Allée, where there is thought to have been a serious slaughter of those retreating, since many relics of soldiers' accoutrements were discovered on that spot in recent times, as if from the remains of soldiers buried in their fighting gear. The two main highways intersecting the plateau were then, as now, the St. Louis Road and the Ste. Foye Road, the former having more of a winding course, before the Grande Allée became a direct prolongation of St. Louis Street. The rock exposures reveal the argillaceous schists of the Silurian Period, whose weatherings have sometimes been productive of dangerous landslides around the face of Cape Diamond, where the crevices, being filled with the slaty detritus, have suffered expansion, and have often thrown the outhanging strata off their balance down on to the lower levels. The height of the rock near Cape Diamond proper, on which the Citadel stands, is a little over three hundred feet, while the highest point of the Buttes-à-Neveu, or Perreault's Hill, is over four hundred feet above the level of the river.

Where Wolfe Died Victorious. It is mentioned in Col. Bouchette's *Topography* that one of the four meridian stones, put in place at Quebec in 1790, stood in the angle of a field redoubt, where General Wolfe breathed his last, thus verifying the exact position where the hero lay when the rout took place. This redoubt, whose ruins were removed when the jail was being built, was one of two redoubts which must have been erected by the British military authorities later than 1759, the other being situated a little beyond Maple Avenue on the St. Louis Road.

William Pitt. There were two English statesmen of this name who left the mark of their genius upon their country's prestige among the nations—namely, William Pitt, the elder, who became the Earl of Chatham, and William Pitt, the younger, second son of the former. It was in 1755, upon the breaking out of the Seven Years' War, that William Pitt, the elder, assumed the leadership of the House of Commons, and became Secretary of State. Two years afterwards he was forced to resign on account of the king's opposition to his measures involving the re-organization of the British army and navy. It was on his return to office, that he became known as the "Great Commoner," from his resoluteness in thwarting the alliances of France against Frederick of Prussia, and in maintaining the efficiency of the British arms on land and sea. By relieving Frederick of the care and expense of keeping up his garrisons in Western Germany against France, by capturing Canada, by upholding Clive's conquests in India, and by virtually sweeping France from the seas, Pitt became the greatest states-man in Europe of his day. When George III came to the throne, Pitt and the Earl of Bute, who was the king's favourite, were not at one on many public questions. Pitt's energetic military meas-ures became obnoxious alike to "Farmer George" and his prime minister, and the "Great Commoner" resigned two years after the death of James Wolfe out at Quebec. We all know the story of his rheumatism and gout—how his greatest mental activity seemed to come to him while he was racked with pain, and sank within him during his years of relief by medical treatment. Nor is that remarkable scene connected with his last speech, denunci-atory of the mistaken policy that had led to the Declaration of In-dependence in the American colonies, ever to be forgotten, in which his dying words were uttered in the hearing of the nation from his place in the House. At the close of his speech he fell back in his seat in a swoon, and a week afterwards his genius and fame were commemorated by a public funeral, in which his remains were carried to Westminster Abbey. He died in 1778.

The Pompadour Regime. The Treaty of Aix-la-Chapelle, in 1748, left the prestige of France somewhat discredited among the na-tions. In Canada she was allowed to hold Cape Breton, and to rebuild Louisbourg. Then occurred what has been called the succession of a young mistress to an old priest, when Louis XV came to the French throne. This young mistress was Madame

Pompadour, who rose to power and retained it for twenty years
—a period in which France sank lower and lower in the scale of
political influence—a period in which the forces that finally made
for the Revolution began to seethe and find increment to their
strength. During this period, up to 1774, the profligacy of court
life, and the ruin of ·the nation's financial credit in France became
the scandal of the world, and little wonder was it that the repre-
sentations made of the peculations and profligacies of Bigot in
New France, should have been ignored by those whose conduct
he was only imitating. This was the age in which John Law had
launched his scheme of a nation paying its debts with paper money
and of Mississippi Bubbles—an age when the king forgot how to rule,
as he ran into the wildest courses of open dissipation and spend-
thriftism, and left his concubines to make and unmake ministers,
to undo treaties and to take their part in war counsels, amid a
public revelry of loose statecraft and court extravagance which
could not go on for long without bringing wrath and ruin in its
wake—as it certainly did. Pompadour died in 1768; Louis XV
died in 1774, and the French Revolution was inaugurated in 1789.

The Bigot Venality. The lesson given in Old France by Pompadour was not lost on New France and its profligate Intendant;
the worthless Bigot. Of all the officers sent out from France for
the government of New France, the Intendant had the best opportunity of enriching himself. The office was of Richelieu's origina-
tion in France, before it was created in the colonies, and involved,
at first, a mere supervision of public works and a general collection
of taxes. But by the time the office was created in Quebec,
its functional pretensions had expanded into a control over nearly
every branch of the public service—political, judicial, and ecclesiastical. And in the case of Intendant Bigot it is difficult to say
where his official duties in the colony began and where they ended.
In his case, he seemed to be co-equal with the governor, presump-
tious enough at times to interfere in military affairs. And as the
Pompadour-Louis carnival of profligacy in France was the prelude
to the after carnival of bloodshed around the guillotine, so the
shameless conduct of Bigot and his creatures was but the prelude
to the bloodshed on the battlefields of New France, and the final
change of masters in Canada. The story of this consummate
libertine has been told again and again. His Intendant's Palace

has disappeared, with only a remnant of its walls dovetailed into the walls of the brewery at the foot of Palace Hill; but the antiquarian, historian and novel-writer have been busy with his *reputation mauvaise;* and the low esteem in which his name and fame is held to-day is akin to that in which his infamies were held by his contemporaries. He had been sent out to America as a government official in Louisiana and afterwards at Louisbourg. He came to Quebec in 1748, under the auspices of Pompadour herself, it is said; and, before he was in the city a year, he had inaugurated the Pompadour system of making and unmaking all public policies in the interest of the individual and the personal. To suit his purposes, he soon had the son of a cobbler for his Secretary, the son of a butcher for his Commissary-General of Supplies; the husband of one of his female favourites for Town-Major; and by-and-by his iniquitous *La Friponne* (the Knave) had been established as a general store, in which the inhabitants of the town were made to trade, irrespective of the exorbitancy of the charges, where goods were sold twice over to the government by a sort of legerdemain business-tact on the part of Clavery, with the connivance of Estèbe, the royal store-keeper. And this is how the machine was kept in motion. Bigot, as Intendant, had the power to sanction or alter the prices attached to all goods imported from France for general use, and had likewise the supervision of the currency. He had become imbued with John Law's idea that paper money was as good as gold, and that if commodities for domestic use were made to go up in price for the sake of increasing the profits from their sale, a more plentiful issue of due-bills, promissory notes, and depreciated papers would keep the pot boiling as long as he—the Intendant of New France—had control of affairs. There was a winking all round at the game—from Vaudreuil, the governor, to Bréard, the Comptroller-General, with a consequent degeneracy in every branch of the public service. Bigot was undoubtedly a sleeping-partner in the operations of *La Friponne*; and when the public service was in need of supplies, these had to be bought from the company's store. But that is not the worst of it. Bigot has the record so far against him as to prove that he was wont to order limited supplies from France for the public service, in order that the public service would have to make their purchases from *La Friponne.* Has there been anything like that since in Canada?

The State of Society Then.   If the condition of France in Pompadour's time showed, in emphatic colours, the lowest degradations from poverty and vice alongside of the flaunting extravagances of favouritism and lewdness, something of the same kind was to be seen, on a smaller scale, in New France under Bigot's Intendancy.   The French officers in the army give us full information of the straits of the colony, in their reports to the home officials.   There had been a storing up of cereals and other supplies previous to 1758, and this, with the heavy exportations of flour from Cadet's and Péan's mills, brought about a scarcity which, from a shortage in the harvest of that year, developed into a famine.   "The people are perishing of want," says one of these reports. "The Acadian refugees, during the last four months, have had no other food save horse-flesh and dried fish, instead of bread.   More than three hundred of them have died of starvation.   The Canadians have only a quarter of a pound of bread per day.   Horse-flesh is six sous per pound.   A soldier receives half a pound of bread a day, and his weekly allowance of other food is reduced to three pounds of beef, three pounds of horse-flesh, two pounds of peas, and two pounds of dried fish."   And this was the year before Wolfe arrived with his army, with a deepening of the gloom all around among the homes of the poor, and even in the barracks of the ordinary soldier—starvation stalking round while a rich storage of cereals lay in the cellars and outbuildings of *La Friponne.* And the contrast to all this is to be seen in the chambers of the Intendant's Palace, at the *soirees* of Cadet, Péan, Déschenaux, or out at Charlesbourg amid the orgies of the Chateau Bigot, where there was no lack of anything even to the point of luxury.   Montcalm once made a jest of his poor provender while he was furbishing up his army to withstand the English invaders, claiming that horse-flesh graced every item in the bill of fare.   But Bigot indulged in no stint of meats or wines at his feasts.   Reckless extravagance, gambling and immorality followed him wherever he went to entertain or be entertained.   It was all of a piece with what was going on at home in France; and when it is known that in one transaction alone—the purchasing of a cargo of general supplies for the public service—a profit of twelve hundred thousand francs was realized by Bigot and his accomplices, there is no shock in the proven charges against them when they returned to France in

1760. Money was plentiful with all of them—the low-born para-
sites and flatterers, as Sir James LeMoine calls them—inasmuch
as the amount realized from their peculations in one year, or rather
in two transactions, was twenty-four million francs. And the
most of these moneys which the "ring" secured, were chiefly
drawn from the coffers of the army—the soldiers being even without the necessaries of life, while the king was being charged for
supplies of food, clothing, ammunition, and war equipment which
never were delivered, and while the soldiers were buying, at their
own cost, the necessaries thus provided for them by the king.
Who was this king of France who was thus robbed? It was Louis
XV, and his leading *dame de théâtre* was Madame Pompadour.
Who was the robber? François Bigot, and his chariot leader was
Madame Péan, née Angelique de Meloises, the wife of his Town-
Major.

The Surrender of Quebec. After the retreat from the battlefield, the French generals who had not followed the mortally
wounded Montcalm into the city, came together within the horn-
work out at Ringfield, not far from the bridge of boats. Vaudreuil and Bigot were both present at the conference, which was
held in a house within the circumvallation. There were different
views expressed at that meeting, some contending that there was
nothing for it, save the surrender of the whole country. Could the
city expect to hold out against the victorious British army? Was
it possible to rally the remnants of the French army, who were
rushing for refuge once more behind the ramparts of Beauport?
Bougainville's detachment was within a mile or so of Quebec;
there were other detachments of French troops at Point-aux-
Trembles. Should they all muster at Cap Rouge and await the
arrival of De Lévis from Montreal? Would it be possible to risk
a second battle before the city was all but destroyed by bombardment? Whatever was said at the meeting, or whatever were the
instructions which Vaudreuil sent to De Ramézay, the commandant of the city garrison, it is known that a retreat was determined
upon, to take place during the night time and along the highways
leading towards Jacques Cartier (now Pont Rouge). The retreating army crowded into that village on the 15th of September,
and two days after, its command was assumed by De Lévis from

Montreal. The Chevalier de Ramézay, left with an increased garrison of nearly two thousand men, took counsel with his officers, and, finding from them that the new elements of his garrison refused to continue willingly under arms, in face of the lack of accommodation, scarcity of provisions and ammunition, and impending bombardment, decided to approach the enemy with a proposal of capitulation. This capitulation took place on the 18th of September; and ever since, the question has been disputed whether the Chevalier was justified in the step he took. Bigot, in one of his letters, written a month later, says he was in favour of renewing the battle the day after the defeat, and Vaudreuil also afterwards publicly expressed his surprise at the action of De Ramézay; his report in November containing these words: "After the affair of the 13th, we marched with the army to the relief of Quebec; but this place capitulated on the 18th, in spite of the succours which I had commenced throwing into the city and the letters which I had written to the Commandant." And between the Governor's advice and the Commandant's act of surrender, there is space enough for much disputation, which is never likely now to be settled. There was nothing in the terms unreasonable either to demand or to grant—including, as they did, the honours of war for the troops, immunity from distraint on the property or interference with the religion of the people; provision for the care of the sick; and a surrender of the guns, ammunition and public stores to the victors. The terms were signed by Admiral Saunders, General Townshend, and Commandant de Ramézay.

The Surrender of the Country. Three different English armies were on their way to Montreal from different quarters in the month of September, 1760. Their object was to enforce the surrender of that place. Colonel Haviland was coming down the Richelieu, Murray was going up the St. Lawrence, and Amherst was on his way from the west. The frowns of discontent on the faces of the *habitants* were beginning to melt into something like a smile of welcome, as these three armies approached Montreal to deliver them from the thraldom of war and the Bigot gang of thieves. Captain Knox, who was with Murray on his triumphal course westward, tells us: "The people brought us horses, some saddled for our officers to ride, others to draw our artillery and baggage. A

curé came to his door, and, saluting us, called out that we were
welcome; while men and women lined the roads with pitchers of
milk and water for the soldiers." Nowhere along the river were
the people unwilling to supply the soldiers with fresh vegetables
and meat, when once they knew that foraging in the English army
was punishable by death, and that all they had to do was to take
the simple-worded oath: "We do severally swear, in presence of
Almighty God, that we will not take up arms against King George,
or his troops, or subjects, nor give any intelligence to his enemies,
directly or indirectly." Nor was there anything of a serious interruption to any of the three armies. They were all in touch
with Montreal about the end of August—Haviland at Longueuil,
opposite the town; Murray on the north-eastern limits, and Amherst on the Lachine side. By the eighth of September the negotiations were brought to an end by the signing of the deed of capitulation of Montreal and the surrender of the whole country by
Governor Vaudreuil to General Amherst. No synopsis of that
document can give a right view of the situation; it should therefore be read in its entirety. In announcing the event to the British
War Office, General Amherst refers to General Murray and Colonel Haviland as having followed his instructions to the very
letter. To the three armies he gives the highest credit for zeal
and bravery, and claims that neither by them nor their Indian
allies was there a peasant, woman, or child injured, nor even
a house burned, from the moment he had entered the French
country. On the other hand, General de Lévis, writing from
Rochelle in the November following: "All that I had to do with
the capitulation was to protest against it for the treatment of the
regulars under my charge, who merited more attention from M.
de Vaudreuil and more respect from General Amherst."

The Treaty of Paris. This treaty was consummated at the close
of the Seven Years' War, on the 10th of February, 1763. The
consenting parties were Great Britain, France, Spain and Portugal. There were twenty-seven articles in it altogether, only three
of which refer to affairs in Canada. Article 4 cedes the whole of
Canada to England, with the exception of the two little islands,
St. Pierre and Miquelon. "His Britannic Majesty," this article
says, "agrees to grant the liberty of the Catholic religion to the

inhabitants of Canada; he will consequently give the most effectual orders, that his new Roman Catholic subjects may profess the worship of their religion, according to the rites of the Roman church, as far as the laws of Great Britain permit." All French-Canadians are to be allowed to sell their estates in Canada, provided it be to British subjects, and to emigrate from Canada without hindrance of any kind, save for debts or criminal prosecutions. Fishermen of French citizenship will retain the right of fishing within the three miles' limit in the waters of the Canadian seaboard, with the privilege of drying their fish on the shores of Newfoundland. St. Pierre and Miquelon are conceded to France as a shelter for such fishermen, though no permission is granted to fortify these places nor have on them more than a guard of forty police. It is interesting to note that in addition to these terms of this famous treaty, Britain also acquired from France several of the islands of the West Indies, notably St. Vincent, Tobago, and Dominica; and from Spain, Florida, and the possessions south and south-east of the Mississippi. As one of the bulwarks of Canadian progress and liberty, the Treaty of Paris, in its Canadian articles, was a direct outcome from the struggle on the Plains of Abraham.

The Monument to Wolfe and Montcalm. The suggestion on the part of the Earl of Dalhousie to have a conjoint monument erected in Quebec to the memories of Generals Wolfe and Montcalm, was of the statesmanship which has prompted Earl Grey to promote the movement in favour of a conjoint battlefield park on the Plains of Abraham. The inauguration-meeting in connection with the former enterprise was held in the Chateau St. Louis; and in a fortnight's time the subscriptions to the expense fund were sufficiently large to justify the laying of the foundation stone of the monument on the 15th of November, 1827. The structure was completed in the following year, and ever since has stood as one of the most prominent historical landmarks in the city. How true reads the monolith at the base of the obelisk, which is sixty-five feet from the level of the Governor's Garden—" Valour gave them a common death, history a common fame, and posterity a common monument." The other monuments connected with the battlefields include, the one to Wolfe at the head of Wolfe Avenue, and the one out on the Ste. Foye Road, to those who sacrificed their lives in the attempt to re-take Quebec. This latter monument was erected by the St. Jean Baptiste Society in 1860, on the hundredth anniversary of the battle of Sainte-Foye. The statue of Bellona, which surmounts the memorial pillar, was presented by Prince Napoleon. At the corner of St. John Street and Palace Hill, there is to be seen the painted image of General James Wolfe. The effigy is made of wood, and is the second of the kind that has found a place there. James Thompson in his diary tells us how it came to be there at first: "We had a loyal fellow in Quebec, one George Hipps, a butcher, who owned that house at the corner of Palace and John Streets, still called 'Wolfe's Corner,' and as it happened to have a niche, probably for the figure of a saint, he was very anxious to fill it up, and he thought he could have nothing better for it than a statue of General Wolfe. At last he found out two French sculptors, who were brothers—of the name of Cholette, and asked me if I thought I could direct them how to make a likeness of the General in wood. Accordingly the Cholettes tried to imitate several sketches I gave them; but they made but a poor job of it; for the front face is no likeness at all." The effigy had quite a number of mishaps, one of these involving its being carried off by some madcap midshipmen on a voyage across the Atlantic, to be brought back again and restored. It is a wonder it stood wind and weather so long, the day of its first seeing the light of the public street having been as far back as 1828. The present effigy was placed *in situ* by the late Mr. John Jones, two or three years before he died. To add to the antiquarian interest of the affair, it may be said that the original niche was filled by a figure of St. Jean Baptiste, and that there is a clause in the title deeds of the property in question making it incumbent upon the owners to see that there is such an effigy of the General preserved on its façade for all time. A bronze statue of Montcalm is to be erected somewhere in the new park. The Hébert statues of Wolfe and Montcalm and Lévis, in the niches of the façade of the Parliament Building, are of the highest art of the sculptor, and two of them are reproduced in half-tones for the illustrating of this volume.

Where Montcalm Died. A little steep-roofed house stood, within the recollection of the writer, all but opposite what is now the last of the very old buildings of St. Louis Street, at the outlet of Garden Street. The architecture of it was much the same as the one still standing. This was the house of Dr. Arnoux, who attended the Marquis de Montcalm on his death-bed. Montcalm's own residence was on the ramparts, and no one can now tell whether, before his death, he was carried thither or not. The general belief is that he expired in the house of his physician, and that from it his remains were carried across to the Ursuline Convent, where they were buried in a rude coffin, hastily made out of rough boards procured by the inmates of that institution. Within the precincts of the Ursuline Chapel his dust mingles with the dust of others, while on the wall may still be read the eulogium of the hero penned by Lord Aylmer, and duly inscribed in marble.

Montcalm's Beauport Headquarters. The "lang toun o' Kirkaldy" is no marvel for its length compared with the long town, or village, of Beauport. It had its origin in 1627, when Robert Giffard became its first settler, and also its first seigneur. The manor-house of Beauport was the home of the Duchesnays for over two hundred years, and it was here where Montcalm had his headquarters during the campaign which ended with his death. The house was still standing in 1879, when it is supposed to have been set on fire by some one who had a grudge against the proprietor. The spot on which it was built is of the greatest interest, as a standpoint from which the environs of Quebec may be surveyed, as well as for its history. No visitor should think he has "done" Beauport without visiting La Canardière, the De Salaberry Monument, the picturesque glen of the Beauport River, the Duke of Kent's Lodge, the Natural Steps, and the trouting pools of De Sable.

The Fortifications in 1759. It is not an easy matter for the visitor-student to identify, from amid the overgrowth of modern improvements in Quebec, the location of her early means of defence. The two main batteries of the upper town were where one of them is to-day, with the other in the old citadel overlooking Mountain Street. In addition to these, there were batteries all along the river front; the first, immediately at the base of the landslide called the Queen's Battery; the second, at the King's Yard, where the government marine steamboats now lie; the third, the Royal

Battery, at what is now the western end of Dalhousie Street; the fourth, the Dauphin's Battery, near where the Grand Trunk Terminal has its site; the fifth, on the ground now occupied by the Custom House; with four more on the shore line leading towards the fortified boom across the mouth of the St. Charles, which was moored near where the present railway bridge now spans the river into Limoilou. On the walled side of the town, facing the Plains of Abraham, there were five bastions; the first, called Cape Diamond Bastion, near where the extension of the Dufferin Terrace now ends; the second, named La Glacière Bastion, near the head of what is now called Citadel Hill; the third, the St. Louis Bastion, opposite what is now the Quebec Skating Rink; the fourth, on the site of the modern Kent Gate; the fifth, the St. John's Bastion, to the right of St. John Gate. Near where the Methodist Church now stands, stood the King's Redoubt, overlooking St. John Street and the approaches to Palace Gate.

The Rigours of the Campaign. Much has been written condemnatory of the cruelties practised by both armies; and, naturally enough, the worst of these have been laid at the door of the British. Wolfe in his manifesto promised the non-combatants that neither their persons nor their property would be molested as long as they remained neutral. This demand for neutrality was, however, not respected by the *habitants* or peasant farmers; and the rangers and light infantry of the British army, with the example of the French-Indian allies before them, indulged in excesses which often were all but uncontrollable. These rangers, whose function it was to make skirmishing excursions apart from the operations of the main army, were, for the most part, Anglo-Americans inured to the mode of warfare of the Indian tribes of the New England colonies; and it is painful to narrate that they did not refrain from the scalping of the French whom they found with the Indians, as neither did the French refrain from scalping the English surprised in their excursions. The property of those who had joined Montcalm's camp at Beauport was specially signalled out by the destroying hands of these guerillas. The name of one Alexander Montgomery, an English captain, has been specially held up for execration by certain French historians; and, if all that has been reported against him be true, the execration is in no way misplaced. At St. Joachim, he is said to have put to death and scalped his captives with the most heartless cruelty. Nor has Captain Starks escaped reprobation for like offences. It is idle, however, for any one to lay the blame of these outrages on General Wolfe. For instance, one historian assures his readers that "Wolfe fell upon the country parishes, indulging in his ravages during the night time to avenge himself for the checks he had received," whereas it was only by way of reprisal against those who had refused to respect the neutrality urged upon them from the first, and had joined the Indians in their mode of warfare against the outposts of the British army, that these cruelties were practised; and it is known that the English general was not personally responsible, but rather discountenanced the inhuman methods of the rangers, whenever he had a chance. The deserters from Montcalm's army, on their return to their farms, were specially marked out for punishment of this kind, their farm-houses being too often destroyed, and they themselves with their families driven into the forest lands surrounding the "clearings," for a place of retreat until the rage of war had spent itself. How these things happened is fittingly represented in the account given by a French narrator of what befell the village of Pointe-aux-Trembles early in the campaign. "At half-past three in the morning," says this writer, "twelve hundred men made a descent on the village, and were received by the fire of about forty savages, who killed seven Britishers and wounded as many. The soldiers surrounded the house near the church and made a number of prisoners, of whom thirteen were women, ladies of the city who had retired to the place for refuge. The prisoners were treated *with all possible consideration.* General Wolfe headed the troops, and M. Stobo was there also. But that which was most lamentable was, that, while the English caused no injury to be done, the savages plundered the houses and stole the property of almost all the refugees." Afterwards, as things turned out, the ladies were set ashore, and the sick and wounded in the melée unmolested, even the prisoners of the male sex being given their liberty. What would have happened had the rangers been the invaders, unrestrained by military authority, it is easy to surmise, considering the license which these gentry indulged in on both sides whenever the chance came their way. The blame of these outrages lay primarily with the calcitrancy of the *habitants*, yet even that cannot justify the conduct of such men as Captain Montgomery and Captain Starks, whose cruel reprisals certainly ought to have been placed under the ban by decree of court-martial, and would no doubt have been, had Wolfe survived. It is but right to say that Captain Montgomery was no connection of Richard Montgomery of 1775 fame, who at the time was serving as a British soldier, under General Amherst, in the Lake Champlain region. General Murray has been blamed, as groundlessly as was General Wolfe, for the cruelties practised during the first winter he spent in Quebec. The skirmishing parties he sent out during that season were not for foraging, but for the checking of approaching skirmishers from the upper reaches of the river. And, when De Lévis was forced by circumstances to retreat from Quebec, the French-Canadians were so humanely treated by the English soldiers, that they were not afraid to return to their places of abode with whatever property they had been able to secrete for the time being in the remote forest lands. They were not long in learning that the soldier who molested them in their occupations, would be treated as a common criminal. Indeed, they became more afraid of the French rangers, who not unfrequently made raids upon the renegades, as they called them, for having submitted to the English so readily. An instance of this is given in the case of a French-Canadian who was caught taking over from Levis a boat-load of provisions for the English garrison. "There," exclaimed the Frenchmen who had seized him and inflicted sundry slashes from their sabres on his person, "go and inform the fine English general of the manner in which we have used you!" General Murray himself, in summing up the whole question concerning the charges of cruelty urged against the English army, gives point to what has already been said in this note in regard to the balancing of the blame for such cruelties. Such cruelties were committed on both sides, and they cannot be relieved of blameworthiness. "Mr. Wolfe," he says, "after warning the Canadians, chastised them for not returning to their houses and quitting their arms. Mr. Monckton, rightly considering that the conquest of the land, if bereaved of inhabitants and stock, would be of little value, gave them the strongest assurances of safety, and even encouragement, if they submitted. The country was yet but partially conquered, and it would have been impolitic to crush the inhabitants." And thus it may be seen, that those who were punished for not abiding by the terms of the compact—and these were exceptions—had no case against those who inflicted the punishment, however much the humanity of these present times may reprobate the severity of such punishment and the cruelties of war. While Murray was getting his garrison under control, two women and a man were whipped through the streets of Quebec for selling intoxicating drink to his soldiers, contrary to regulation. If there had been no regulation in the one case, and no well-known compact in the other, there might be some reason for accusing the English General of injustice in the severity of the punishment administered, but not otherwise, considering the cruelties that were countenanced by war in these earlier times. During Murray's first winter there were many instances of retaliation on the peasantry who had disregarded the edict of neutrality. The property of those who had left home to join De Lévis at Montreal was destroyed, no communities being so harried by Murray's light infantry as the parishes between the Chaudière and the Etchemin Rivers. And Murray himself tells us why this was done, even in face of his own desire not to have it done. These inhabitants, as Dr. Miles says, had harboured detachments of the enemy's troops on various occasions, and more particularly when hostile movements were made in the direction of Point Lévis, and lower down on the south shore. Other reasons assigned for the punishment inflicted upon them were that they had tried to raise a general revolt throughout the Quebec district against the British; that they had sent all their young and able-bodied men to join the French troops; and that in other respects they had disobeyed the English governor's orders, and neglected to attend to the regulations he had established with reference to non-combatants and their families. In addition to this, the local authorities in these districts had been sending in false reports about the antipathies of the inhabitants towards the English, and of the assistance rendered in supplies of meat, grain, and farm-yard produce which had been promised to De Lévis and his troops on their descent against Quebec, as soon as the winter months had passed.

The British Soldier and the Canadian Winter. There is still one sentry's post in the Quebec Citadel which is pointed out as the

16

coldest place for a sentinel in North America. This is not now true for Canada, which has in these later days extended its boundaries to higher latitudes where the services of the soldier are required. In 1760, General Murray's men found the climate one of their severest trials, and Knox tells us, in his journal, what a grotesque appearance they had to assume when out on grand parade in their improvised winter's garb. The inventions to guard against the cold, he tells us, were various beyond imagination. "They resemble rather a masquerade than a body of regular troops. Men cannot recognize familiar acquaintances, and movements are always hurried. The sentries are relieved every hour; and, to enable the men to move about with facility, mocassins and snowshoes have been ordered for all, as well as *creepers*, to be attached to the heels of their boots. And yet, notwithstanding all precautions, men and officers are frost-bitten by the hundred in their faces and limbs." One of their great hardships during that first severe winter was the drawing of wood from the forests in the outskirts of the town. "Whenever a milder day comes," says Knox, "two subalterns, four sergeants and two hundred men do all the fatigue duty within, all the rest of the garrison being off duty cutting and sleighing wood. This question of firewood became the all-engrossing object of attention. Each party could make only one trip a day to the forest, returning with a moderate load on a wood-sled, dragged by hand. The men were impeded in their movements by having to go armed, and to keep a good lookout for fear of attacks by Indians skulking in the neighbourhood, covering parties of light infantry being sometimes detached for the protection of the wood-cutters." And notwithstanding all efforts at protection from the cold, as many as a hundred cases of frost-bite would occur in a day.

The St. Charles's Bridge and Plain. The windings of the St. Charles's River, from its outlet from Lake St. Charles to its entrance into the St. Lawrence, are perhaps more pronounced than in any other stream in the world, unless it be the Forth in Scotland. The wide plain which it waters has been a garden for Quebec, spread out, as it is, in all its rural interest to one travelling along the Ste. Foye or Little River Roads. The stream has five miles of its windings to overcome before it reaches the steep rock at Indian Lorette—

The laughing lyric of the lake's first-born,
As leaps it from its earlier creeping pace;
Wayward, eddying here,
Madcap, rushing there,
Bellowing between the scooped-out rocks
Only to run calm and clear again
Across the farmer's well-ploughed lands.

And what an historic interest there is about its lowest windings from its Scott's Bridge, round by the Victoria Park, under its Park Bridges and the Bickell Bridge, and thence under the Dorchester Bridge, and the Railway Bridge! The river was crossed by a ford between the old boom and the bridge of boats, and the identification of the historic points around—of Jacques Cartier's first winter's camping ground, the Jesuits' Monastery, the Recollets' Convent, Ringfield, the Intendant's Palace, the King's Storehouse, and other scenes of past events—makes the lower reaches as attractive, historically speaking, as are its higher reaches for their rural picturesqueness.

The Modern Overgrowth. The exploitation of the new park threatens many of the modern surroundings of the Plains of Abraham with extinction. The two main thoroughfares remain intact. The only fortifications guarding the battle sites are the *Martello Towers*, which were completed in 1812 at a cost of sixty thousand dollars and after six years spent in their erection. They were erected under the supervision of Sir Isaac Brock, the hero of Queenston Heights. To examine any one of the three of them left is to examine them all. Though not all of the same size, they are of the same plan. The sides facing towards the west are thirteen feet thick, diminishing in thickness until they come to be only seven feet on the side facing the city. The lower flat of the structure was set aside for tanks and storage; the second for the accommodation of the men of the garrison in charge; and what may be looked upon as the roof of the round structure, was intended as the place for the heavier guns, protected as it is only by a wooden awning. Since the departure of the British troops these outposts from the Citadel have not been garrisoned. Besides these, the modern overgrowth includes many public institutions, such as the Franciscan Church and Nunnery; the Church of England

Female Orphan Asylum; the St. Bridget Asylum; the Ladies' Protestant Home, the Jeffrey Hale Hospital and its Mackenzie Wing; the Church and Monastery of the Franciscan Monks; and the Jesuits' Church and Retreat. Between the Buttes-à-Neveu and Maple Avenue, the overgrowth is not likely to suffer any check until the grounds whereon occurred "the thickest of the fray" are crossed with the lines of suburban streets lined on both sides with dwellings, for the citizens who delight in the *rus in urbe*, when selecting their place of residence.

Admiral Sir Charles Saunders. The record of Sir Charles Saunders is one which places him in the forefront of the naval officers who sustained, under Lord Anson, the glory of England's navy during the Seven Years' War. He was with Anson on his famous voyage round the world, with the stout ship *Centurion* for the flagship of a fleet of five smaller vessels. The voyage was made up of secondary events and only one Spanish vessel was taken; but it assured the supremacy of the seas to Britain, won by a long line of navigators from Blake's to Saunders's day. The latter was promoted to a captaincy on his return, being then only thirty years of age; and when Anson assumed control as First Lord of the Admiralty, there seemed to be to him no one in sight as competent as Charles Saunders to take charge of the British fleet in its expedition against Quebec. Saunders had worked his way up, having been appointed treasurer of Greenwich Hospital in 1754, and Comptroller of the Navy in 1755. When he set out for Quebec, the fleet under his command comprised no less than forty-nine vessels of all kinds, having on board 13,750 men, including soldiers and marines, with two thousand pieces of ordinance. The tonnage of the whole fleet put together did not amount to much more than the tonnage of two of our modern-day Dreadnoughts. It was a large armament, however, for these times, comprising a little less than a third of the whole British fleet, and the cost of it absorbing a little more than a third of the whole national revenue for the year. Without the co-operation of the fleet there could have been no capture of Quebec; but that is very different from saying that Wolfe was secondary to Saunders, or that the largest share of the victory was due to the latter. Such discrimination is entirely out of place, as has been the folly of trying to give General Townshend the largest share of the renown won on the battlefield. Saunders was a sailor of the highest repute, and the brilliant part his ships played in the bombardment of Quebec, was duly recognized amid the joy of the nation, and fittingly rewarded by the king. In 1760, Admiral Charles Saunders became Lieutenant-General of Marines; in 1765, a Lord of the Admiralty; and in 1766, First Lord of the Admiralty. Previous to his expedition to Quebec he had been elected to Parliament. His death occurred during the December of 1775, while the British national eye was again turned to Quebec, to watch the outcome of the Montgomery siege.

Institutional Overgrowth. The Plains of Abraham are topographically indicated, in their more assured scope, by the sites which have been selected by certain religious and charitable institutions for building purposes. The visitor, while learning the lesson of the battlefield proper, usually halts to identify these institutions; and it has been thought advisable to add to these miscellaneous notes the following paragraphs concerning the same:

The Jeffrey Hale Hospital. On the line of Claire Fontaine Street, already spoken of as the Buttes-à-Neveu, are two spacious institutions that immediately overlook the scene of the second contest; the one more remote from the Grande Allée being the Jeffrey Hale Hospital, with its McKenzie Wing and side-hospital for infectious diseases; and the other facing the Grand Allée, being the Franciscan Church, with its Nunnery. The Jeffrey Hale Hospital had its early home near the foot of Glacis Street, having been founded in 1865 by the citizen whose name it bears, and having been moved to its present site in 1901. The McKenzie Wing was built in terms of the bequest of Mrs. Turnbull, wife of Colonel J. Ferdinand Turnbull, and daughter of the late James McKenzie, and was opened in 1906. The institution has a training department for nurses, and all the appliances of a well-equipped hospital. The view from its outer gallery is perhaps the most engrossing to be seen from any part of the city. In addition to the Hale-Turnbull bequests, it has an endowment from the bequests of the late Senator J. G. Ross. The guns in front of the building were presented by the federal militia department. There has been spent on the institution over half a million of dollars. Near it formerly stood one of the four Martello Towers.

The Church and Convent of the Franciscan Nuns. This institution had its origin in 1892. From very humble beginnings, it has grown to be one of the most attractive edifices in the city. It is in charge of what are popularly known as the "White Nuns," the chief function of the organization being, within, the perpetual Adoration of the Blessed Sacrament, and, without, the care of the sick and afflicted. The order is of modern date, having been founded by Madame de Chappotin. The mother society at Rome has already the supervision of fifty houses such as that in Quebec, with over two thousand *religieuses* attached. In the Quebec house there are over one hundred nuns and novices, many of whom are sent from time to time to foreign countries to enter upon their professional duties. The church is among the most conspicuous points of interest in the city, standing as it does on the edge of the famous battlefield, and being in its interior as choice a piece of church ornamentation as is to be seen anywhere. The service is specialized by the responses of the nuns in a body before the altar. The prospect from the tower of the church gives a full panorama of the city and its battlefield environment.

The Church of England Female Orphan Asylum is a large and somewhat gaunt-looking building of gray stone, standing on Grande Allée on the western slope of the historic Buttes-à-Neveu. It was originally a military home for discharged soldiers' widows and orphans; and, when the British troops left Quebec, the premises became vacant, and, being purchased in 1873 under Anglican auspices, were utilized as the present Female Orphan Asylum. It has an ample endowment, drawn for the most part from the sum allotted to the charities of Quebec by the liquidation trust of the Quebec City Savings Bank. The institution is in the hands of a matron and preceptress, under the authority of a committee of ladies of the Church of England. Not far from it is one of the Martello Towers, overlooking the Cove Fields.

The St. Bridget's Asylum lies further west on the Grande Allée, at the corner of De Salaberry Street, and stands where the final shock of the battle of 1759 took place. The institution had its origin in 1856, in a small building near St. Patrick's Church, within the walls. It was inaugurated under the auspices of the St. Patrick's congregation, by whom the present edifice was erected.

The function of the institution is to educate orphans and give a shelter to the aged and indigent of St. Patrick's parish. It is under the management of the Sisters of Charity, acting with the St. Patrick's Ladies' Charitable Association. The endowment is small, and consequently its grant from government has to be largely supplemented by donations from the charitably disposed. There is a neatly arranged chapel in connection with the institution. The singing of the orphans of a summer's evening or a Sunday morning has a very grateful effect on the listener outside, and gives an incidental charm to the whole historic neighbourhood. The grounds behind the building are known as the "Cholera Graveyard," where is to be located the meeting-place of the two armies in 1759, with a thicket in its rear from which the French scouts annoyed the English army on its way towards what is now the line of De Salaberry Street. The rout of the battle emanated from this piece of ground, which was afterwards used as a burial place for the victims of cholera, when that dread disease visited Quebec in 1832, 1849 and 1854. It is now a recreation ground for the inmates of the asylum.

The Ladies' Protestant Home is situated a little further west on Grande Allée, on the opposite side from St. Bridget's Asylum. It was opened in 1863. Eight years previously there had been organized in the city the Ladies' Protestant Relief Society, and a successful appeal to the public led to the society's incorporation and the erection of the present spacious edifice. The institution is under the supervision of a matron and a committee of ladies selected from all the Protestant denominations in Quebec. The finances have been greatly relieved by donations from the Senator Ross Bequest, and others bequeathed by Mrs. Colonel Turnbull and Mrs. G. R. Renfrew. The function of the institution is the safe-keeping of indigent old women and the up-bringing of female orphans. The grounds of the institution were the scene of the dash of the Louisbourg Grenadiers and of the fatal wounding of General Wolfe before he was borne back to where his monument now marks the place where he expired.

Battlefield Cottage. This is now the property of the Dominican Fathers, who came to Canada in 1873, and established themselves at St. Hyacinthe. They are known as the "Friar Preachers."

Their residence and adjacent chapel are on historic ground, the well, from which was drawn the water to moisten the lips of the dying general, being in the rear of the latter. The Fathers came to Quebec as late as 1906, under the oversight of a native of Quebec, their superior.

The Merici Convent, with its farm-like surroundings, is situated further out on the St. Louis Road, having for a western boundary-line the highway leading to Wolfe's Cove. The estate was once the property of the Gilmours, and went by the name of Marchmont up to the time when it passed into the hands of the Nuns. A number of battlefield relics have been dug from the grounds adjacent to the Convent, and it was in the south-west corner of this property that Verger's outpost was established.

The Findlay Asylum is situated on the Ste. Foye Road, between De Salaberry Street and Maple Avenue. The institution sprang from very humble circumstances. The first donation towards its organization was eight hundred dollars—"the orphan's mite" as it was called—donated by a certain Miss Finlay to the Anglican Bishop of Quebec. The money was expended by the Bishop in the purchase of a cottage on Sutherland Street, near Mount Pleasant; and, in 1861, a further donation of two thousand dollars, given by another lady, induced the Anglicans of Quebec to assist the Bishop in putting up the present building. The place, as at present organized, is a home for male orphans and indigent old men. It enjoys a comfortable endowment received from the Ross Bequest, and is conducted under the auspices of the rector and church-wardens of the English Cathedral. From the site on which the institution stands must have been witnessed the rush of some of the French forces in retreat towards Genevieve Hill and St. Roch.

The Franciscan Church and Monastery. These are situated on the northern side of the plateau further west and down from the Ste. Foye Road, overlooking the valley of the St. Charles. Under the supervision of these friars a school has been established in Montcalmville.

The Jesuits' Church and Monastery. These are further to the westward on the Ste. Foye Road, the latter being near where the skirmishers came out of the woods to turn the flank of Townshend's division, to be met with in turn by a flank movement on the part of Townshend.

The Laval Normal School is on the line of St. John Street where that thoroughfare coalesces with the Ste. Foye Road, a few yards beyond the city limits. The function of training teachers is confined to male students. The old home of the institution was on the site of the Chateau Frontenac. Behind it is Sauvageau Hill, which witnessed the cruelties of the Indians on General Murray's men, as they retreated from the Battle of Sainte-Foye.

NEAR WHERE MONTCALM DIED

Historical Placing
of the Event

Historical Placing of the Event

To study an event in history aright, one has to place it in proper relationship with the collateral events in the world's history; otherwise, as is the case in many of the pages of our colonial histories, events may be thrown out of proportion. As has been claimed, the capture of Quebec in 1759 was a world's event, the direct outcome of the momentous struggle for supremacy among the nations of Europe during the Seven Years' War. That war has been briefly referred to in a note in a previous part of this volume, in which only a few of the more prominent actors in that struggle could have a place—a note intended as an incentive to the reader to place the Siege of Quebec in right relationship with the other events of these early times. The story of Britain's rivalry with France, during the middle of the eighteenth century, finds its complementary counterpart in the story of the rivalries between the French and English colonies in North America; and the latter story can hardly be properly understood without a grasping of the more prominent details of the former. The record of both stories in parallel lines has, perhaps, yet to be drawn up, with a converging point in the event which forms the subject of this volume. Meantime, no one will be inclined to deny that there is ample justification for classifying the change of Imperial masters in Canada as an event of world-wide importance—in fact, the Greatest Event in the History of Canada.

In presence of the prowess of Frederick the Great, the two more prominent reigning sovereigns in Europe, at the time this event occurred, were George II of England and Louis XV of France. The worthlessness of the latter's character gave not only immoral countenance to manifold irregularities of administration in France, but encouraged in their downward gait the band of weaklings and reprobates who had been put in charge of the fiscal affairs of New France. Cardinal Fleury was the king's prime minister up to 1743; but, after his death, the youthful monarch gave even a looser rein to his folly, joining with his frivolous and corrupted court in a course of profligacy and dissipation that had its counterpart, if on a very much smaller scale, in the immoralities openly indulged in, within the purlieus of Montreal and Quebec, by Intendant Bigot and his shameless associates. It was the age of Madame Pompadour—an era that made France a byword in the hearing of the nations, and brought New France to financial ruin. During the twenty years of her open and unblushing ascendancy over her royal paramour, she made no secret of her aspiration to be a sort of prime minister in her own right, making a scandal of the king's administration in nearly every undertaking affecting the nation at home and abroad, and bringing a shrug of shame from every right-minded Frenchman. Indeed, if one would read aright what was happening during her day in New France, he may readily enough find it depicted on a large scale in the condition of affairs in old France. The country was in the hands of a profligate tyranny. Taxation for personal selfish ends knew no limitations. The upper classes, who shared in the "boodle," were given entirely up to vice and frivolity. Industry was at poverty's door, with nothing before it but additional burdens, starvation or death.

And, at last, as if the bankruptcy of the coffers of the Court was only a thing to be laughed at, Pompadour would have her war—her very own war; for had she not received, to the pluming of her feathers, a personal condescending letter from no less a royal personage than Maria Theresa of Austria, calling her "dear cousin" in it, and begging her to use her influence with the king to come to the support of an alliance against Frederick of Prussia, on account of his refusing to abide by the terms of the "Pragmatic Sanction?"   And when that alliance was consummated, through such an unseemly channel, ·the nation had no option but to take up the additional burden of the expenses of the Seven Years' War—a war which eventually led to the humiliation of France to the rank of a second or third rate nation, and of New France to its exit from the rank of French crown colonies altogether. Truly, the frivolous administration in France, with Madame Pompadour virtually at its head, had but a grotesque look in presence of the European statesmanship of a Frederick the Great of Prussia, or of a William Pitt, the Great Commoner of England.

Not to travel too far afield, the British government in 1756 made the declaration of war against France which brings us in full view of North America as the seat of the war that was to settle the great colonial question, which the Treaty of Aix-la-Chapelle in 1748 had by no means finally settled. That question was, who should hold the suzerainty of the country between the Gulf of Mexico and the northern seas? France presumed to lay claim, by right of discovery, to the whole of the continent, with the exception, perhaps, of the New England territory, and the lands east of the Alleghanies. Naturally enough, the disproportion in the populations of the two nationalities led New England to set aside such a claim, remembering, no doubt, that John Cabot, under the auspices of Henry VII, had raised the British flag on the shore of Cape Breton, nearly forty years before Jacques Cartier raised his cross on the Gaspé coast. At the time of the opening of the Seven Years' War, there were in America twice as many English colonists as there were French, and four times the wealth in favour of the former. Charlevoix had evidently his eye open to the contrast between the two peoples when writing his history; and, in the matter of going to war, he tells us that while the Anglo-Americans did not desire war, because they had much to lose, nor meddled with the savages, because they did not think they required them; the French Americans detested a state of peace, and liked to dwell among the natives, whose admiration they gained in war, and their friendship at all times. This eagerness to find occupation in warfare had no doubt much to do with the building of forts along what was called the "debatable territory," each of which has its own story in Canadian history. In the taking and re-taking of these forts, the English and French colonists alike won an intermittent renown, until finally the struggle culminated in the victory of General Montcalm at Carillon, on the shore of Lake

Champlain. Indeed, that victory had its share in giving point to the demands of the people of England for a firmer hand at the head of state affairs in London, with a change of commanders for the American seat of war.

While France was masquerading under questionable petticoat government, it has to be said that England was also wilting and drifting under the Duke of New-castle's administration. Macaulay tells us how that nobleman, when in difficulties, went about chattering and crying, asking advice and listening to none. And, when the people of England were told to their face, by more than one of their pamphleteers, that they were a race of cowards, submitting, as they were doing, to an enervating rule that was bringing their country to the disgrace of effacement by the French in Europe and America, the diatribe became unbearable, when the news was carried to London of Admiral Byng's misfortune in the Mediterranean, and General Aber-crombie's repulse at Ticonderoga. And during the crisis in public opinion that followed, the eloquence of William Pitt, calling the nation to its sense of duty, rang out in the House of Commons, supplemented, as it was, by the rhetoric of Charles Fox and his Tory associates. The whole nation was disturbed. The breath of revolution was in the air. The foreboding of Walpole on his death-bed, concerning a possible change of dynasty, was re-called. Charles Stuart, the "Young Pretender," against whom Wolfe and Townshend and other young officers of rising fame had been gaining experience under the fiery Duke of Cumberland, was still alive. Another Culloden, re-versed as to its results, might have to be fought, un-

17

less the king delivered himself from his drivelling ministers. In a word, the whole people were aroused. From every nook and corner of the kingdom came the demand that something be done—with every eye, be it said, turned on William Pitt as the man through whom amelioration might come. "I am sure I can save the country, and that no one else can," he was reported to have said; and, when the people were irresistibly ready to take him at his word, the king was forced to send for him to form a ministry.

Pitt had never been a favourite with the king, whereas Newcastle had been; and, when the new ministry was finally formed, a place had to be provided for the latter. William Pitt, however, was Premier, being Secretary of State and leader in the House of Commons. And, in two or three of his delightfully concise and pithy paragraphs, Lord Macaulay gives us the following glimpse of how events in America took their place within the programme of events, which made a prestige for Britain that has been hers ever since, while contending with the nations in their rivalries and ambitions:

"The first measures of the new administration," he says, "were characterized rather by vigour than by judgment. Expeditions were sent against different parts of the French coast with little success. The small island of Aix was taken, Rochfort threatened, a few ships burned in the harbour of St. Malo, and a few guns and mortars brought home as trophies from the fortifications of Cherbourg. But soon conquests of a very different kind filled the kingdom with pride and rejoicing. A succession of victories undoubtedly brilliant, and, as it was thought, not barren, raised to the highest point the fame of the minister to whom the conduct of the war had been intrusted. In July, 1758, Louisbourg fell. The whole island of Cape Breton was reduced. The fleet to which the Court of Versailles had confided the defence of French America was destroyed. The captured standards were borne in triumph from Kensington Palace to the city, and were suspended in St. Paul's Church, amidst the roar of guns and kettle drums, and the shouts of an immense multitude. Addresses of congratulation came in from all the great towns of England. Parliament met only to decree thanks and monuments, and to bestow, without one murmur, supplies more than double of those which had been given during the war of the Grand Alliance.

"The year 1759 opened with the conquest of Goree. Next fell Guadaloupe, then Ticonderoga, then Niagara. The Toulon squadron was completely defeated by Boscawen off Cape Lagos. But the greatest exploit of the year was the achievement of Wolfe on the heights of Abraham. The news of his glorious death and of the fall of Quebec reached London in the very week in which the Houses met. All was joy and triumph. Envy and faction were forced to join in the general applause. Whigs and Tories vied with each other in extolling the genius and energy of Pitt. His colleagues were never talked of, nor thought of. The House of Commons, the nation, the colonies, our allies, our enemies, had their eyes fixed on him alone.

"Scarcely had Parliament voted a monument to Wolfe, when another great event called for fresh rejoicings. The Brest fleet, under the command of Conflans, had put out to sea. It was overtaken by an

English squadron. Two French ships of the line struck. Four were destroyed. The rest hid themselves in the rivers of Brittany. The year 1760 came; and still triumph followed triumph. Montreal was taken; the whole province of Canada was subjugated; the French fleets underwent a succession of disasters in the seas of Europe and America. The French had been beaten in 1758 at Crefelt. In 1759 they received a still more complete and humiliating defeat at Minden.

"In the meantime, England exhibited all the signs of wealth and prosperity. The merchants of London had never been more thriving. The importance of several great commercial and manufacturing towns, of Glasgow in particular, dates from this period. The fine inscription on the monument of Lord Chatham in Guildhall records the general opinion of the citizens of London, that, under his administration, commerce had been united and made to flourish by war."

In the biographical notes which follow, the history of the times is further lit up with the personal. The miscellaneous notes fill out the details of the main event. The king of France sent out Montcalm, De Lévis, Bougainville, and others of his army, tried and efficient officers, to take charge of military affairs in New France, with the meagrest provision, however, for the upholding of them in their campaigning. These men's achievements are worthy of respectful record within the hearing of every Canadian, be his mother-tongue English or French. The king of England sent out Amherst and Wolfe, with their veteran-trained armies bountifully equipped, to check the encroachments of the French prestige in America; and the record of their deeds also illuminate the story of Canadian warfare in the "debatable territory." From Louisbourg to Michillimackinac, the bravery of both French and English soldiery, volunteers and regulars, was put to the severest test. Their deeds of valour made for a building up, though they did not always know it, not for overthrow. Their antagonisms, as we still ponder them, rectify the Canadianism that continues to throb for the welfare of the Empire, sowing seeds of the pacific in its patriotism, and a blending of purpose in its nationalism.

Tracing the final issue of the cession of Canada from the suzerainty of France to British Imperial protection, one cannot but wonder how things would have turned out, had there been no Pompadour to wink at the rascality of a Bigot, or had the shambling Newcastle not been superseded by the indefatigable Pitt. The people of Quebec have wisely eliminated all overestimating of the victory or defeat on the battlefields near their door. The prestige of the British Flag is now theirs to prize and celebrate. The names of Wolfe and Montcalm are now emblems of peace, not of war; and the proof of this is to be met with under the shadow of the monument erected to the twain of them on one spot and under one pyramidal shaft. Yea, the lives of these heroes and their comrades survive, to bless the common citizenship in a country that would seek its destiny through the divinity of peace rather than through the passions of war.

Place Names

As a further assistance to the reader anxious to make sure of his ground while studying his lesson about Quebec, it has been suggested that an alphabetical list of the Place Names that occur in connection with the campaign of 1759-1760, should be given a place at the end of such a work as this, with an explanatory note connected with each. The following list is therefore added, though it must not be supposed to include every name, but only the more prominent:

Ange Gardien is seven miles from Montmorency, and **Chateau Richer** seven miles from Ange Gardien. They are both thriving French-Canadian villages, possessed of not a little romantic charm for the tourist as he passes through them, on his way to Ste. Anne de Beaupré. They have each their own story to tell of the incidents of Wolfe's attack on Quebec, in which they had a share, and the stories are not without a record of cruelties perpetrated against their inhabitants before and after the "Battle of the Plains."

Basilica, The, stands at the head of Fabrique Street—the beginning of one of the two main thoroughfares of the plateau of Quebec. The foundations of the church were laid in 1647, by Bishop Laval; the first mass was celebrated within it by Father Doucet in 1650, and the consecration services held on the 18th of July, 1666. It was restored to its present form after the Siege of 1759; the grouping of the buildings in its vicinity including the Seminaries of Laval, the Bishop's Palace, and the Presbytery. The interior of the church was completely gutted during the bombardment by Admiral Saunders, the adjacent seminaries also suffering seriously at the same time. The Basilica is built on the site of the Chapelle de la Recouvrance of Champlain's time, erected to commemorate the restoration of Canada to the French in 1632.

259

Beauport is perhaps the longest village in the world, and its main street is by no means void of interest to one taking a highway drive to Montmorency Falls. The largest institution along the line of the highway is the Beauport Asylum, which had its origin in 1845, when Dr. James Douglas, father of the author of "Quebec in the Seventeenth Century," joined with Dr. Morrin, founder of Morrin College, in asking the government to favour the plan of having the asylum for lunatics erected outside the city, and in such a healthful and isolated situation as the village of Beauport. The institution is under the supervision of the Sisters of Charity, who are provided with a staff of medical attendants and male overseers. The provincial government pays for the support of the inmates at so much per head. The modern methods of treatment have happily been adopted, and cases of cure are being reported from time to time. The buildings have had three records of fire, the last and most serious of these occurring in 1890, when the most heart-rending scenes were witnessed, as the doubly demented patients, threatened by the flames, made frantic efforts to escape from the corridors and windows. The institution is situated in the midst of a woodland picturesqueness which enhances the historic interest attached to the locality. Only a short distance from the asylum is the site of the Giffard House, the headquarters of General Montcalm and Governor Vaudreuil in 1759. At the mouth of the Beauport River was one of the strongest of the French redoubts. Lake Beauport is ten miles or so from the village of Beauport, back in the Laurentides.

Belmont Cemetery is about half-way between Quebec and the village of Ste. Foye. The portion of ground comprising its terraces was originally purchased from the farmer who owned it, by the fabrique of Notre Dame, Quebec, in 1857. It is the burying ground connected with the Basilica and St. Jean Baptiste Churches. The entrance to it is indicated by a spacious gateway on the right-hand side of the Ste. Foye Road, as one drives from the city, while the centre of the cemetery is marked by a high iron cross, from which the various pathways lead. The tomb and monument of the historian F. X. Garneau are to be found in this cemetery, the latter having been erected through the liberality of the citizens in 1867. (See Biography of General Murray.)

Bellevue Convent, on the Ste. Foye Road, has a striking appearance, as seen from the highway; and from its windows a magnificent view of the surrounding country is to be had, and of the immediate site of the battle of Sainte-Foye. The earlier owner of the lands on which it stands was the wealthy citizen, Mr. James Gibb. The building was erected in 1872, under the auspices of the Congregation de Notre Dame de Montreal, being one of the many convents established all over America by that organization.

Calvaire is a lakelet of over a mile long, which gives its name to the rural hamlet near the river. It is a charming summer's retreat, with approaches to it that have their picturesque surprises at every turn of the roadway. The locality is of historic note in connection with the campaign undertaken by De Lévis in the spring of the year 1760.

Cap Rouge is nine miles or so from Quebec, and may be reached by either of the two main highways from the city. On the bluff overlooking the village, near the end of the great railway span, and within the grounds of Radcliffe, is the site of Roberval's encampment when he wintered in Canada in 1543. Jacques Cartier had preceded him, spending a winter here in 1541, at a spot near the shore of the river. Near by, on the levels above, was Bougainville's camp, commanding the road to St. Augustin and Pointe-aux-Trembles, and thence to Three Rivers and Montreal.

Charlesbourg, the nestling village seen from any of the city-outlooks towards the north, as occupying the slope of the valley of the St. Charles, five miles away, was originally known as Bourg Royal, and is mentioned as a place of resort in the early days of the colony. In the retreat from the Plains of Abraham in 1759, a large number of Montcalm's soldiers sought refuge for a time near Charlesbourg Church.

Chateau Bigot, now in ruins, may be reached by the Charlesbourg Road, or by a pathway that diverges from the Beauport Road near the Lunatic Asylum. It has long been looked upon, by antiquarian and novelist, as the scene of many of Bigot's debaucheries; though it has recently been affirmed that, as a summer's residence, it was built by Intendant Bégon, and that a confusion in the pronouncing of the names led to its identification as a rural retreat of Bigot and his loose companions, where they might hide away for a season from their civic responsibilities. The place is often spoken of as Beaumanoir, or the Hermitage.

Chien d'Or, The, was the name given to the buildings that once occupied the site of the present post-office, the first of the three being in existence at the time of the Siege of 1759. The effigy and inscription inserted in the façade of the present building is supposed to commemorate the rascality of Bigot and his *La Friponne*, one of his victims being supposed to have had the satirical verse cut into stone—which, being freely translated into English metre, is as follows:

> I am the dog that gnaws a bone,
> And, while I gnaw, I'm all alone;
> The time will come that's yet to be,
> When him I'll bite who now bites me.

And we all know how the profligate Intendant of Quebec was eventually bitten for his misdeeds.

Citadel, The. In thinking of Quebec, as it was in the time of Wolfe and Montcalm, there should be no identifying of the Citadel, as it was before the Siege of 1759, to what it was subsequently or what it is now. The French Citadel was lower down, nearer the levels of the Place d'Armes and the outworks from the old Chateau St. Louis. Indeed, the old fortifications, even to the walls, were all changed, when the Duke of Wellington, as Premier of England, decided to modernize them more in line with what they are to-day.

Claire Fontaine Street, the street of the "clear fountain," takes its name from one of the springs found along the rising ground of the Buttes-à-Neveu. Like De Salaberry Street, it has also a history of its own, inasmuch as it is the line of land along which Montcalm marshalled his army, on the morning of the "Battle of the Plains."

De Salaberry Street, which was named in honour of the hero of Chateauguay, whose statue is in one of the niches in the façade of the Parliament Building, has a fame all its own from having been the line of land where the final shock of the "Battle of the Plains" took place.

Dorchester Bridge, which crosses the River St. Charles at the end of Bridge Street in St. Roch, was constructed in 1822. It still retains the name given to its predecessor, which was opened in 1789, to supplant the bridge of Montcalm's time. Before the Siege of 1759, there is said to have been regular ferry communication from the one side of the river to the other near the site of the present Marine Hospital building.

Esplanade, The. The open space which extends from St. Louis Gate to Kent Gate, has witnessed many proud pageants and gay military reviews under imperial and federal rule. It was reserved as an open space for drilling purposes for many years previous to 1759, having around it still the Old Government House, the Garrison Club, the Anglican Bishop's Residence, and the Church of the Congregation.

Grande Allee, The, extends from St. Louis Gate to Maple Avenue, the name indicating its early origin as a favourite drive to the outskirts of the town. In its modern aspects, it recommends itself as one of the best laid out of the city streets, the grading and paving of it having been ordered by Sir François Langelier, when he was mayor.

Hotel Dieu, The, or Convent of the Sacred Heart, situated on Palace Street, played a part in the Siege of 1759. Although sorely shattered during the bombardment, it was placed at the disposal of General Murray for a time as a hospital for the wounded of both nationalities after the battle. The institution had a very humble beginning in 1639, through the philanthropic enterprise of the Duchess d'Auguillon, who secured a deed of the land on which it stands from the "Company of One Hundred Associates." The Duchess and her uncle, Cardinal Richelieu, later on, endowed the institution; and with the revenues derived from this endowment and from the properties which have since come by grants and legacies into the hands of the community of the Hospitalières, who control its affairs, the hospital has grown to its present dimensions and palatial importance. The chief function of the institution is to care for the indigent sick. Its medical appliances are of the most advanced scientific type, and both rich and poor are now received as patients within its walls. The relics of the chapel include the bones of Father Lallemont and Father Brebœuf, the Jesuit martyrs of Canadian history.

Intendant's Palace, The, was situated at the foot of Palace Hill, remains of the building being still enclosed within the precincts of Boswell's Brewery. It was a spacious building, extending over what would constitute two or three blocks, with nearly five hundred feet of building-length upon it, and including a frontage that ran towards the St. Charles, and was laid out in *parterres* and garden walks. (See note in Montgomery Siege.) The name lingers in the district, which is still spoken of as the "Palais." The *Palace Gate* stood about half-way down Palace Street. The remains of the old French gate were removed in 1791. The gateway removed in 1874 was only about forty years old when it was dismantled. The site of it is easily identified, since it stood between the Hotel Dieu and the end of the Arsenal or Cartridge Factory.

Jesuits' College, The, which so long went by the name of the Jesuits' Barracks, and concerning which General Murray had to put up with so much obloquy, stood on the site now occupied by the Hotel de Ville, or City Hall. The front of the building, being in line with the street, sloped upwards from Fabrique Street, the incline detracting somewhat from the architectural look of its massive quadrangle. The history of this site forms a central thread in the history of the city itself, and appropriately has it been converted into the *plaisirs* of the City Hall. In 1637, the Jesuit Fathers, who had their headquarters at first opposite what is now the Victoria Park, obtained from the company of New France a grant of twelve acres of ground in the city on which to erect a seminary, church, and residence. The foundations for the main building were laid in 1647, and of the chapel in 1650. The latter must not be confounded with the old Jesuit Church that once stood at the corner of St. Anne and Garden Streets, and which was all but destroyed during the Siege of 1759. In 1720 the college was rebuilt; and in 1773 the Order was suppressed by papal decree, nine years after their contingent in Quebec was recalled. On the reorganization of the Order, the Jesuits returned to the city in 1842, taking up their quarters on Dauphine Street, where the Church of the Congregation, the residence of the Fathers, and Loyola Hall now stand. The religious operations of the Quebec branch of the Jesuits know no abatement, and large crowds of the citizens still frequent their celebrations of the several church fêtes. The old college building was demolished in 1873, a year or two after the British troops had been withdrawn from Quebec. In 1760 it had been first used as a magazine and military storehouse, but in 1765, General Murray had it fitted up as a barracks, and the court and garden laid out as a parade ground.

King's Wharf, The, is approached from Champlain Street through the archway of the Old Arsenal, or King's Storehouse. It was opened in 1821. On the opposite side of the Cul-de-Sac was situated the King's Storehouse of the French period, and near it was one of the batteries of lower town that made reprisal on the town of Levis and Holmes's vessels during the Siege of 1759.

La Friponne, Bigot's warehouse, the byword in Quebec in the years previous to the arrival of Wolfe, was situated at the foot of Palace Hill, near the corner of St. Nicholas and St. Valier Streets. The name, which simply means "the place of cheatery," is vividly described in the novels of Joseph Marmette and William Kirby. The retail shop, which opened immediately on the street, and to the east of the Intendant's residence, or palace, was kept by one Clavery, the clerk of the Royal Storekeeper; but this was only used as a blind to the wholesale knavery carried on in the larger warehouses behind.

Laurentides, The, or Laurentian Hills, form the northern background of the picture of Quebec. They are a distinct range of themselves, having been identified by Sir William Logan as the oldest of all our geological formations. They consist of hornblendic and micaceous gneiss, interstratified with irregular beds of crystalline limestones, and bed-like masses of magnetic oxide of iron and other economic ores. The prominent peaks, as seen from Quebec, are the cone-like Hills of Laval, which run in a continuous range towards Cape Tourmente; the two heights which form together a miniature Ben Lomond, the one being called Valcartier Mountain and the other Mount Pinckney; and, away to the left, the more moderate height of Bonhomme. A drive across the highways intersecting the range reveals romantic scenery of the most attractive character—a blend of hill and dale, of woodland lakes and rushing streams—unsurpassed in any part of the province.

Laval University is an outgrowth from the Laval Seminary. Both exist contemporaneously, the latter having been founded as early as 1663, the former having received its charter in 1852. The Seminary buildings suffered seriously from the bombardment of 1759.

Levis, the town which lies opposite Quebec, took its name from the Marquis de Lévis. At the time of the Siege of 1759, it was but a scattered series of settlements, which have since developed into the villages of Lauzon, Bienville and South Quebec, or Point Levis, and the parishes of St. Joseph and St. David, besides the town proper. It is said that in 1759, the Church of St. Joseph was converted into a hospital for the wounded, General Monckton himself having been conveyed to his camp near by it to recover from his wound.

Lorette. There are two villages which go by this name borrowed from Europe, namely, Lorette Ancienne and Jeune Lorette. The former, which is near the middle of the valley of the St. Charles, shared in the excitement connected with De Lévis' concentration at the Ste. Foye Church. The latter is better known as Indian Lorette, on account of its being the latter-day home of the Hurons.

Monuments. The monuments connected with the events of 1759-1760, are Wolfe's Monument raised on the Plains of Abraham; the Wolfe and Montcalm Monument, in the Governor's Garden; and the Monument-aux-Braves out on the Ste. Foye Road. These all bear their own record.

Orleans, The Island of, is a favourite resort for Quebecers in summer. It is twenty miles long and five miles broad. The building near the wharf is the Chateau d'Orleans, or Island Hotel, while at the other extremity of the village, on sloping ground, is the parish church of St. Petronville de Beaulieu. In summer there is regular ferry communication between the Island and the city. The Indians called the island *Minigo.* It was partly explored by Jacques Cartier in 1535, and by him was called *Isle de Bacchus,* on account of the wild grapes his sailors found on it. A year after, it received its present name in honour of Philippe de Valois, Duke of Orleans, and son of Francis I. In 1656, it was occupied by six hundred· Hurons, the greater part of whom were massacred one May morning by their enemies the Iroquois. Five years after, it was again over-run by the Iroquois, when a party of Quebec sportsmen, including Governor Lauzon's son, were cruelly put to death. Before the capture of Quebec in 1759, it is said to have been peopled by two thousand settlers. Wolfe's soldiers landed at St. Laurent on the main channel, and took possession of the island as a means of getting at Quebec by way of Montmorency. The English fleet lay in the deep channel opposite where the hotel now stands, and the swift current that prevails there was utilized, on the advice of Bigot, it is said, to send fire-ships amongst them. The island is divided up into six parishes—St. Pierre, St. Famille, St. François, St. Jean, St. Laurent, and St. Petronille. As a side trip from Quebec, a visit to the island, and a day or two spent at its comfortable hotel, is an experience the visiting tourist should not miss; and, if opportunity arises, a drive through the parishes, or a sail from the one watering-place to the other in any of the little river steamers, might be profitably taken.

Parliament Building, The, was commenced in 1878 and finished in 1887. Its predecessor, which was transferred to the provincial government in 1871, stood on what is now called Frontenac, or Montmorency Park, at the head of Mountain Hill. The present site is said to have been covered with a thicket of oak and maple at the time of the Siege of 1759, near which General Montcalm was seen, by his retreating comrades, to be seriously wounded, before passing through the old St. Louis Gate.

Péan's House, Madame, is supposed to have been situated at or near 56 St. Louis Street, but in order to learn who Madame Péan was, beyond being Angelique de Meloises in her younger days, and a well-known Quebec belle of Intendant Bigot's time, reference must be made to William Kirby's famous novel of *Chien D'Or*.

Perrault's Hill is the more modern name given to the highest point on the Grand Allée, which is spoken of in history as the Buttes-à-Neveu. It received its later name from the well-known Quebec philanthropist and educationist, who had his residence near by in the Asyle Champêtre, that was destroyed by fire a few years ago.

Ramparts, The, or the street overlooking the Louise Basin, extends from Port Dauphine Street to Palace Street, having on its line the battery of upper town, where 'stood the old French Battery of 1759.

St. Augustin is situated near the shore of the St. Lawrence, thirteen miles from Quebec and three from Belair. It is in the county of Portneuf, as is also Pointe-aux-Trembles. There are villages of the same name at the centres of both of these parishes, the churches being the crowning architectural feature of both. The latter has historic interest not only from Wolfe's campaign of 1759, but also in connection with Benedict Arnold's invasion of 1775.

St. Charles River, which rises in Lake St. Charles, about fifteen miles from Quebec, and which still goes by the name of "Little River," forms the northern limit of the city. It received its name from the Recollets in honour of M. Charles de Boues, a benefactor of their order. It had been called "The St. Croix" by Jacques Cartier, since he landed near its mouth on the 14th of September, 1535, "the Day of the Exaltation of the Cross." Going further back, its Indian name was "Kahir-koubat," meaning "winding stream." The sylvan scenes along its banks are very enchanting, as one follows it all the way from the Lorette Falls, and along its main tributaries.

St. Louis Gate, the spacious archway which makes of St. Louis Street and the Grand Allée a truly royal avenue, replaces the earlier narrow gates of 1694, 1791, and 1823. The corner-stone of the present structure was laid by Lord Dufferin, the year he retired from the governor-generalship.

St. Roch existed as a suburb of Quebec previous to 1759, though between it and lower town there was no properly laid out street connection until about the beginning of the last century. Beyond the Intendant's Palace there extended, previous to this, the open space called *La Vacherie*, or pasture-land for the city cows, extending all the way from Côte St. Genevieve to the St. Charles. Two devastating fires have swept St. Roch—the first two occurring in 1845, and the second in 1866.

Spencer Wood, the residence of the governors of the province, ..
is situated in the midst of a woodland environment, wherein Bougainville took up his position with his men, after the retreat of
Montcalm.   One of its approaches crosses the Ruisseau St. Denis,
the brooklet which passes by Wolfesfield on its way to Wolfe's Cove.

St. Sauveur, as a suburb of Quebec, received its name in honour
of Abbé Jean le Sueur de Saint Sauveur, a Norman priest who
settled in Quebec in 1638.   The two churches of this district are
respectively known as Notre Dame de Lourdes, distinguished
by the golden effigy on its minaret, and the Church of St. Sauveur,
with its spacious convent and school edifices on either side.

Ursuline Convent.   This has been referred to elsewhere.   The
points of interest within its walls are its chapel and spacious gardens.   It was here where Montcalm was buried, and where his
heart contained in a casket was finally said to have been placed.
The votive lamp in the chapel is said to have been first lit by Marie
de Repentigny in 1717.   Several interesting memoirs connected
with the place have appeared from time to time, and these may
be readily secured on enquiry at the Convent.   The relics are of
ancient date, and the paintings form a valuable collection well
worth examining.

Lightning Source UK Ltd.
Milton Keynes UK
UKHW02f2251230818
327720UK00012B/584/P